◆ ◆ ◆

Praise for *How to Give a Speech*

"For your next presentation, put yourself into the hands of Dr. Gary Genard. Under his wise tutelage, you will learn how to put your speech together, and even better, deliver it as a master speechmaker. *How to Give a Speech* is a tour de force! It provides you with step-by-step support for everything you need to become a powerful communicator."

—JOHN BALDONI
author of *Great Motivation Secrets of Great Leaders* and
Great Communication Secrets of Great Leaders

"An extremely useful resource for anyone who needs to speak in front of groups, large or small. It has helped me speak with more confidence."

—PETER T. SMITH
Region Vice President, The Hertz Corporation

"Although I've been a professional speaker for 13 years, I learned valuable lessons from *How to Give a Speech*. Whether you're a rookie or a veteran, Gary Genard's perceptive, accessible book provides all the tools you need to present with confidence."

—ROBERT SPECTOR
International speaker and author,
The Nordstrom Way to Customer Service Excellence

"Reading *How to Give a Speech* was an eye-opening experience. I didn't realize there were so many small changes I could make when presenting to sound more appealing... starting with how I said my own name and title! Gary Genard is an outstanding coach and he's written a terrific how-to guide to public speaking. Get this book, and recommend it to your colleagues."

—JODI WHALEN
Marketing Director, Food Network

"*How to Give a Speech* has helped me to develop a robust toolbox of speaking techniques. My communication effectiveness has improved significantly as a result of using these methods. I feel even better about my improved self-confidence and focus in knowing how to utilize these tools for any situation requiring effective communication."

—DAVID BEAN
Vice President of Finance, Vertex Pharmaceuticals

"*How to Give a Speech* offers a friendly, engaging roadmap to public speaking. It's an insightful read. Dr. Genard discusses the importance of being honest in your remarks, while maintaining a conversational tone with your audience. *How to Give a Speech* shares invaluable techniques on how to be a successful orator."

—LISA MURKOWSKI
U.S. Senator (AK)

"These techniques work! As a communicator to global audiences, I have found Dr. Genard's tips extremely helpful in achieving clarity and power, and getting my critical messages out. His techniques for relaxation, visualization, and audience analysis have become common practice for me. From speeches to meetings to conference calls, *How to Give a Speech* is a book that has helped improve my communication skills and reduced my frustrations."

—XIAOWEN HEURTEUX
VP/Senior Financial Analyst, Citigroup

◆ ◆ ◆

How to GIVE A SPEECH

◆ ◆ ◆ ◆ ◆ ◆ ◆ ◆ ◆ ◆ ◆ ◆ ◆ ◆ ◆ ◆ ◆

EASY-TO-LEARN Skills for More Successful & Profitable
Presentations, Speeches, Meetings, Sales, and More!

GARY GENARD
Founder and President
Public Speaking International

Cedar &
Maitland
Press

www.cedarandmaitland.com

How to Give a Speech

To order this book, please call (781) 643-6400, or write to:

Cedar & Maitland Press, LLC

1026 Massachusetts Avenue

Arlington, MA 02476

www.cedarandmaitland.com

info@cedarandmaitland.com

Discounts are available for group purchases.

ISBN 978-0-9796314-4-3

Library of Congress Control Number: 2007903307

To Janice and Lydia

Contents

CHAPTER TEN: Nuts & Bolts: Practical Skills for Presenters

Acknowledgments

For their suggestions, guidance, and generosity in lending me some of their valuable time, I would like to thank the following people: John Baldoni, Karma Kitaj, Gretel Hartman, Jodi Whalen, and Christian Koestler.

On Maximizing Your Natural Talents

Be brisk, be splendid, and be public.
— SAMUEL JOHNSON

This book will improve your skills in any speaking situation. It will increase your confidence and charisma. It will improve others' opinions of your character and competence.

But it will do something even more valuable than these important things. *It will dramatically increase your influence with everyone you talk to—about anything.*

Any book that attempts such a task had better focus on your actions as a speaker. By that, I mean your physical behavior and vocal approach that, together, convey messages quite apart from the things you're saying. These are the critical nonverbal components of public speaking, and they are the focus of this book.

How to Give a Speech, then, is a self-improvement book, one that aims to dramatically improve your public speaking *performance*.

Why should you worry about performance? Well, the answer to that is simple. To change people's lives in some positive way—to affect how they think, feel, or act as a result of your presentations—you must perform at the peak of your abilities.

Successful and influential speakers know all about reaching this pinnacle of achievement.

Think of the great orators whose names we honor—people like Pericles in ancient Greece, Winston Churchill, Abraham Lincoln, and Martin Luther King, Jr. Each of them was famous and everyone knew what they stood for. But it was their stirring addresses in public, their moments of peak performance, that secured their places in history.

They consciously used their attributes as speakers to the fullest extent possible. They *performed* at their very best.

How to Give a Speech shows you how to maximize your own natural speaking talents in powerful and specific ways. The type of speech or presentation you give doesn't matter. In each case you have the same task: honest communication that reaches your listeners' hearts and minds, while conveying a clear sense of who you are and what you stand for.

Here, then, is solid hands-on advice delivered in what I hope is a compact and reader-friendly package. You can keep this book on your bookshelf if you like. But I urge you to slip it inside your briefcase, purse, or carry-on and take it with you whenever you know you'll be speaking in public. It truly is a guidebook of dynamic public speaking, meant to be as practical as possible.

There are 75 entries in all, written as one-to-four page "Quick Tips" organized in ten chapters. You can read the book from cover to cover, explore a topic that's on your mind at the moment as a speaker, or head straight to any Quick Tip that catches your eye.

Chapter One, "Calming Your Nerves and Gaining Confidence," offers six ways you can do just that. Chapter Two, "Organizing and Preparing Your Material," shows you how to set a clear purpose for your speech or presentation and then accomplish it.

In Chapter Three, "Twelve Easy Ways to Achieve Presence and Charisma," I discuss a dozen practical methods for making a strong impression on your audiences. Chapter Four, "The Power of Your Voice," focuses on the virtually limitless power of the human voice to persuade and influence others.

Creating "Dynamic Introductions and Conclusions" is the essential topic covered in Chapter Five. Chapter Six, "Delivering Your Critical Messages," shows how you can discuss your product, service, or ideas strategically and powerfully.

Chapter Seven, "Engaging and Motivating Audiences," and Chapter Eight, "Dealing with Skeptical Audiences and Resistance," offer advice on making your presentations livelier, more involving, and more credible for your listeners. Chapter Nine, "Handling Q & A Like a Pro," offers six lessons for improving your skills in question-and-answer sessions. Finally, Chapter Ten, "Nuts & Bolts: Practical Skills for Presenters," provides a dozen tips for dealing with the challenges that speakers regularly encounter.

How to Give a Speech is the result of my thirty-five years as a professional actor, public speaking professor, and speech coach to clients from around the world. So it's filled with the practical matters these people have told me are on their minds as presenters.

I'd love to hear from you if you'd like to add to the contributions from this speaking community. Or feel free to simply give me feedback on the book. If there are topics that you'd like to see covered in future editions, I'd be delighted to hear about them.

Now my last word to you before your valuable speech or presentation, is the traditional lovingly intentioned advice from the world of the theater: *Break a leg!*

With best regards,

Gary Genard
gary@garygenard.com

CHAPTER 1

Calming Your Nerves
and Gaining Confidence

◆ ◆ ◆

"The mind is a wonderful thing.
It starts working the minute you are born and never
stops until you get up to speak in public."
— ROSCOE DRUMMOND

1 ▸ Got 5 Minutes? — Relax!

"Easy does it."

"Take it easy."

"Easy as pie."

In America, we admire people who not only do things expertly, but who make them seem easy.

I believe one of the reasons we feel this way, is that when things are going smoothly—when we're hitting on all cylinders—we're functioning at peak efficiency. And that just feels *right*.

Some people call this level of performance being in "flow," or nowadays, being in The Zone. Whatever name you attach to it, it's a feeling of effortlessness—an intense pleasure that comes from focusing completely on a task rather than the obstacles in our way.

The first rule of successful presentations, then, is to bring ourselves to such a state of natural relaxation. Once we do that, we can place our focus where it needs to be. And that's on our message and our listeners, rather than on the things that make us self-conscious and anxious.

But given today's hectic professional schedules, we also need a way to help us relax *quickly*. So here's a wonderful way to achieve a productive level of relaxation (this is not an oxymoron!) if you only have 5 minutes to spare:

1. **Find a quiet and solitary place.** (In a pinch, a toilet stall will do, or even your car parked outside your speaking venue.) Sit comfortably, with your feet flat on the floor.

2. **Close your eyes.**

3. **"Listen" to your breath for the first minute.** That is, pay attention to what happens when you breathe in slowly and calmly. Understand with your body, not your mind, how breathing nourishes and sustains you. Feel the breath flowing down your throat, filling your lungs, and then bringing life-giving oxygen to every cell in your body.

4. **Now, focus your awareness on a visual image you "see" in your mind.** Make it a neutral color and shape: a green circle, a yellow square, a blue triangle. Any object that doesn't have emotional overtones for you is fine. (Avoid red as a color.)

5. **See that object in as close to crystal clarity as you can manage.** This will take concentration and a bit of practice at first. As you do, adopt a passive attitude toward any other mental activity. Thoughts, imagery, and feelings will emerge in

your consciousness. Simply notice them then let them go on their way. Keep a gentle yet firm focus on your image. Do nothing; just let your awareness *be*.

6. **Your breathing will become slower and deeper.** This is what you are aiming for. You're now in a calmer and more relaxed state. When you're ready, open your eyes and slowly stand. If you feel any lightheadedness, sit down again, for your body may not be used to taking in this level of oxygen. Once you have it, try to maintain this level of calmness and *relaxed breathing* as you go on with your daily tasks.

This exercise allows you to calm yourself and focus your attention—two critical attributes of a good speech or presentation. Practice it until you can do it easily at a moment's notice, because that's when you will need it most!

 2   From Nervousness to Charisma

Don Knotts was a television comic of the 1950s who was famous for his nervous guy routine. He'd appear in the "Man in the Street" interviews on the Steve Allen Show. This guy would always be a quivering nervous wreck—jiggling legs, facial tics, bulging deer-in-the-headlights eyes. Then he'd reveal his occupation as a brain surgeon or an explosives expert, which was of course hilarious.

When it comes to speaking in public, most of us probably recognize ourselves in The Nervous Guy.

Yet what is perhaps most intriguing about the nerve-wracking aspect of public speaking, is the fact that we *need* some nervousness to be good as speakers. If we're not sufficiently activated, we probably won't come across as the personable, charismatic performer who can reach out and connect with listeners.

Your nervousness as a speaker, then, is a relative phenomenon. Communications researchers estimate, for instance, that only 10-15 percent of the population has severe "communication apprehension," or CA (also known as speech anxiety), at a level that actively interferes with one's ability to speak in public. Most of us just experience the normal butterflies. And that, as Martha Stewart would say, is a *good* thing.

Without those butterflies, we would never feel the need to "psyche ourselves up" for a presentation. We'd feel mellow and completely in control—and we'd almost certainly come across as full of ourselves and boring.

Part of the reason we feel nervous, of course, is because of our desire to be good. And that's just another way of saying we want to *do* good for our listeners. Even though we're concerned about ourselves, we're also thinking of others—in this case our audience members. We instinctively want to succeed in driving home our important message to them.

It is this desire to have a meaningful conversation with our listeners—about something that we know matters to them—that makes us personable and focused as speakers. Embrace that need closely enough, and we soon forget about our own jitters. Keeping our eye on the prize of our critical message—and using all of our awareness and speaking tools to do so—we *appear* more confident about what we have to say. And so we are.

All of this adds up to more charisma in the eyes of our audience.

So don't fear your nervousness. Remind yourself that it's an essential part of psyching yourself up to do a good job. Turn your attention instead to what you need to say and do to convince *this* audience, in this speech or presentation.

Your listeners will not only see you as more personable. You'll also be far more persuasive.

3 ► Create Your Own "Command Performance"

You have a speech or presentation coming up. Naturally, you've been thinking about it. The truth is you've been kind of *obsessing* about it, haven't you?

As the gears have been turning in your head, you've begun to imagine all kinds of things that might happen concerning your performance—some of them right out of a Stephen King novel.

But why do we beat up on ourselves like this? If we're going to spend time imagining scenarios for our upcoming presentation, why not make them *positive* scenarios? Otherwise, we run the risk of creating a self-fulfilling prophecy, with some of those bad things happening because we've really paved the way for them.

So create and internalize a positive outcome to your speech instead. One way to do this is by writing out what I call a "Command Performance Movie." This is simply a way for you to visualize a successful speech before the fact, so it's more likely to come true.

The Command Performance Movie isn't a real movie shot with a camcorder, but instead is a scenario-in-your-own-mind about the good and positive things that are going to occur at your appearance. It should be written out using pencil and paper or a computer keyboard.

Include in your one or two pages your pleasure about speaking at the occasion, the way you accomplish all of your objectives as you go through the speech, the fact that the audience is nodding and paying attention, etc. Also include comments about how everyone seems to perceive you just the way you want them to, personally and professionally. Be sure to put in the specific ways in which you *feel* positive about the experience.

How much detail you include is entirely up to you. That, and the specific items you mention, are only limited by your (optimistic) imagination!

The following is a sample Command Performance Movie. Yours will be different, since it will be unique to your situation and goals. Wherever possible, make your imagined scenario as close to the actual details of the occasion as you can.

◆ ◆ ◆

My Command Performance Movie

Today, I'm giving a 45-minute address at a breakout session at the Mega-Movers of the Universe Convention. I'm dressed professionally, in style with good quality clothes that aren't overly flashy. The audience senses that I'm relaxed, confident, and clearly looking forward to giving my talk and sharing ideas with them.

They can see I'm really enjoying being here with the opportunity to speak. After I'm introduced, I step to the lectern, smile, and nod at the audience. I take a slow relaxed breath, and begin my conversation with my listeners.

I speak clearly and knowledgeably, in an easy, confident tone. My voice is lively and engaging. As I make eye contact with audience members, I see that they're paying attention and look interested. I stay focused on my message, which I know is coming through loud and clear. I know this material and I'm really enjoying getting it across!

When I finish, everyone smiles and applauds warmly. They've clearly enjoyed my speech. As I return to my seat I overhear someone say, "Now *that* was an interesting presentation!" I know this has been a rewarding experience for them *and* me.

4 ▸ Four Key Ingredients to Achieving Influence as a Speaker

The reason we give speeches and presentations, reports at meetings, sales talks and campaign speeches and every other type of public performance, is to *influence* our listeners somehow. Knowing that we can do so should give us confidence. In fact, it should make us eager to get up on our feet!

Following are what I consider to be the four actions on your part that are essential to achieving influence as a speaker. You should, therefore, include them in every one of your presentations:

1. **Establish Your Credibility.** You must have *credibility* in an audience's mind if you are to get listeners to think, feel, or do what you want them to as a result of your speech.

   "Why in the world should I listen to this person?" is the ever-present question in the average listener's mind. It's up to you to supply the answer. And fast: during the first 60 seconds or so of your talk.

   Tell them why they should listen to you—and I mean literally tell them. What is your experience to speak on this topic? What's your job title? How long have you been working (or hobbying) in this field?

   What did you do to prepare for this particular presentation? Unless you're already famous, you must begin to build your credibility from the very first word out of your mouth. Being credible is what makes you worth listening to and believing.

2. **Be Honest.** Sound obvious? Actually, when we lack confidence in ourselves as presenters, we usually try to be something different from what we really are. We wear a mask. Or we slip on invisible armor to protect ourselves. Worst of all, we

try to be "as good as" someone who's a successful speaker.

But none of these solutions ever works, because listeners only pay attention when a speaker is being completely honest with them! Each of us is absolutely unique in the universe—and therefore interesting. It is equally unproductive to try to hide from audiences, and to sound like someone we're not.

To be influential as a speaker, show your listeners your true self.

3. **Connect With Your Audience.** Always remember that when you speak, you are there for the audience's benefit, not your own. Therefore, you need to find ways to put yourself in their shoes, so you can understand and meet their needs.

If possible, greet some of your audience members before your presentation. When you speak, continually look your listeners in the eyes. Some presenters are so nervous that they look over the heads of their audience members. But isn't it easier to speak to other people than to the back wall of a conference room or auditorium?

Equally important: watch your listeners' reactions. That way, you can adjust your style if need be so you'll *always* be connecting with them.

4. **Think in Terms of Action.** Most of us make a pair of mistakes when we give a presentation: (1) we tend to wrap our content around us like a safety blanket, and (2) we keep stepping out of our talking points to wonder how we're doing as a presenter.

This may be a natural reaction, but it places us 180 degrees from where we want to be when we speak. We should be paying attention to the audience, that is, not our content or ourselves. After all, you should know your topic and who you are pretty well. When you're presenting, your objective has to be to get that material and yourself across to your audience!

I said at the beginning of this Quick Tip that the reason we speak is always to influence our audiences somehow. So again, think about what you want your audience to do as a result of this presentation. Exactly how do you plan to change people's lives?

Thinking that way will give your presentation real drive and relevance. It should also remind you of how much your speech really matters.

Now, go influence.

5 ▸ Establishing Rapport with Your Audience

The first 60 seconds of any presentation is a killer, isn't it?

You're nervous. The audience doesn't know what to expect. And everyone—on a bad night, *you* included—is preoccupied with whatever they were thinking up to the point when you started speaking.

So you'd better hurry up and make a strong introduction, right?

Actually, no. That's the mistake too many speakers make. There's an important and necessary part of your presentation that should precede the introduction.

It's called the *greeting*.

One reason a presenter and his or her audience often feel awkward in one another's presence, is because the speaker hasn't taken time to establish rapport with his or her listeners. Which only stands to reason: before you can begin to talk about your topic, you have to acknowledge the people you'll be talking to!

It's in your greeting that you begin to establish rapport, so it can't be left out. This is the moment you introduce *yourself* to your listeners, and vice versa. The fact that you do it verbally and your listeners do it through nonverbal communication, doesn't matter at all.

Here are 5 Steps you should take to gain audience rapport though a well accomplished greeting. Doing these five things will help you not only start out smoothly, but get listeners on your side immediately:

1. **Look at your audience as you walk to the lectern or front of the room, or stand at the conference table.** Nothing complicated here. Just remember Noel Coward's advice to actors, to please remember their lines and not bump into the furniture.
2. **Smile.** Or at least assume a pleasant and *open expression.* It's surprising how many people go through life with a permanent semi-grimace on their face. Why subject your audience to that? Even a eulogy doesn't require an expression of doom, for goodness sake! (Incidentally, I suggest you smile in a conference call too. Your audience will hear it in your voice.)
3. **Greet them.** Say, "Good morning," "Hello everyone," "Wow, did you see that tornado that just blew down the street?," or anything else that fits the situation and/or the mood of the gathering. In a conference call, this is absolutely essential, and often left out.
4. **When you reach the spot you'll be speaking from, continue to look at the audience for two or three seconds.** Build anticipation (and make sure everyone has quieted down).
5. **Introduce yourself—including your title—and reveal your topic.** I tell clients to *re*-introduce themselves when talking to outside audiences, even if everyone present already knows your name and title. Your title is an extremely important part of your credibility, and your listeners need to hear it.

Tell them who you are and what you'll be speaking about today.

Now here's an incredibly important point:

Notice that up until now, you haven't looked at your notes once. Why would you? Presumably, you know who you are and what you'll be talking about during this presentation.

Too many speakers look from the audience to their notes to the audience to the ceiling, etc. etc. when they first start speaking. It's distracting and gives you as speaker no opportunity whatever to establish rapport with your listeners.

Instead, spend ALL your time up to this moment acknowledging and greeting your audience through your eyes, your words, and your actions. It's a pre-Introduction moment that packs a big payoff.

6   **"What Do I Do With My Hands?"**

If there's one question I'm most often asked by people who are self-conscious about speaking in public, it's: "What do I do with my hands?"

The answer is, not much.

Seriously.

Let me explain: People figuratively—and sometimes literally—tie themselves up like pretzels worrying about how they should stand, move, and gesture as a speaker.

I once watched a judge standing in front of an audience settle himself into an odd position with his shoulders, arms, and hands because, apparently, he'd acquired those body parts in the moments immediately preceding his speech and hadn't a clue what they were for.

During the 45 minutes or so that this distinguished jurist spoke, I didn't pay the scantest attention to what he was saying. I just kept staring at him, wondering what gym class had been like for him in junior high school and conjuring up dark reasons why he'd gone to law school all those years ago.

Obviously, if *your* audience is acting like this because of the way you hold yourself when you speak, your influence is not going to be what you'd been hoping for.

So why do so many of us leave our normal physical expressiveness behind when we speak in front of others?

The reason, I think, has to do with *context*. We are usually quite comfortable with our physicality at work and in other everyday situations. But we suddenly become extremely self-conscious when we have to give a talk or presentation. Yet there's absolutely no reason why this should be the case!

What we should aim for instead as a speaker is a kind of blissful ignorance where our bodies are concerned. In other words, we should forget about our hands, feet, and other appendages for a perfectly simple yet solid reason: our audience members haven't the slightest interest in them.

For our listeners as well as for us as presenters, it's all a question of *focus*. If you are utterly focused on your message and getting it across to your listeners, that's all you'll have time for at the lectern or conference table. There'll be no time whatsoever to regret that your hips are wider than you'd like them to be, or that you don't possess Sean Penn's hairline.

If you're uninterruptedly into the flow of your critical points, your gestures will *naturally support* what you're saying.

And it's exactly the same for your audience. When the engine of your speech is running smoothly, your listeners will hear that hum, and they'll be with you all the way. (Of course, a repetitive gesture or odd stance will pull their attention away from your message, just as happened with me when I was listening to the judge.)

Believe it or not, the most natural position for a speaker from an audience's perspective, is with one's arms hanging down neutrally at the sides. The arms and hands can then be brought into play when a gesture is *absolutely needed.*

In other words—gesture when you positively can't avoid it

any longer. That gesture will look necessary and true to your audience.

Try it right now: Stand up, and let your arms hang neutrally at your sides. It may feel awkward at first, but it looks perfectly natural from the audience's perspective. Now start to speak, bringing your hands up to make a gesture only when it feels exactly right to do so.

Therein lies the natural and supported hand movement.

So, here's the General Rule to remember about hands and gestures:

Any movement that reinforces or amplifies your message is okay, and any movement that detracts from your message is *not* okay.

Keep this rule in mind, and you won't find yourself pulling your nose every third sentence, or making uplifting hand gestures that seem to be saying, "I need to throw up, but nothing's happening!"

Now, go forth and gesticulate comfortably and appropriately.

◆ ◆ ◆

CHAPTER

Organizing and Preparing
Your Material

◆ ◆ ◆

▼ 7 ▼

The Step You Must Take Before
Deciding On Your Topic

The phone on your desk rings.

It's the Senior VP of Sales for the Asia-Pacific Region.

"Xavier," she says, "I want to congratulate you on the outcome of the Mega-Mega-But-*Mega* Project. Fantastic job! ... In fact, I'd like you to come out to Los Angeles and talk to my team about it."

Doinng!

Immediately, the thought starts bouncing around the interior of your skull: "*What* am I going to talk about?"

Right?

It's a perfectly natural reaction. When we discover we have to give a presentation of any kind, our first reaction is to start working out the content: Topic, approach, format, stories and examples, handouts, PowerPoint slides, etc., etc.

Unfortunately, it's not the most productive way to approach your challenge *at this point*.

Why?

Because of one simple question: How do you know what you should talk about before you understand what your listeners need to hear?

In other words, when faced with the fact that you must give a talk or presentation—you must start with your audience, NOT the topic.

That's because there are certain critical points of information you need before you can go any further. They include the answers to three questions:

1. **Who** is this audience?
2. **What** information or type of persuasion will they respond to?; and
3. **What's** the best method of giving that to them?

Once you've answered these three questions, you're in a much better position to grasp exactly the kind of information you need to provide, and how to go about it. Otherwise, it's a case of the cart leading the horse. When you've answered those broad questions, it's time to get more specific:

◆ Who is this audience, in terms of demographics, culture, politics, socioeconomic level, and so on? ("Culture" here can mean many things besides nationality or geographic origin. Examples include clubs or social groups, departments within a corporation, religious affiliation, and so on.)

◆ How much information does this audience already have? What do I need to give them that someone else hasn't?

◆ What are their expectations and preferences for this presentation? (For example, military gatherings probably expect to see a PowerPoint presentation; while leadership teams are usually more attuned to a strategic vision than too many details, etc.)

◆ Does the emotional climate of this gathering have some relevance to the presentation? (Examples include recent layoffs at the company, or yesterday's announcement of hugely improved sales for the 4th quarter.) Your audience may be strongly biased toward or against your message due solely to this factor.

◆ Who has spoken to this audience in the past? What did they speak about, and how successful were they in their approach?

◆ What else can my liaison or contact tell me about this audience and the occasion?

By answering these questions, you'll be much better armed as you approach your engagement. You'll be able to put together content that will give these listeners exactly what they need to hear on this particular occasion. And what speaker could expect to do better than *that?*

8 Know Your Purpose and How to Accomplish It

Let's assume that you've followed the advice in Quick Tip #7 on the previous two pages. You have a firm grasp of the make-up of your audience, including their expectations and preferences.

Now you're ready to give some serious thought to what you'll try to bring about with these listeners—in other words, your *purpose* in giving this presentation.

"But," you say, "the purpose is obvious! I've been asked to speak about..."

And that's exactly the misstep that many speakers make. They have confused "purpose" with "topic." Yet the two are very different.

In fact, far too many presentations fail because the speaker has no clear idea of the purpose the speech is intended to achieve.

Your purpose is simply *what you want to accomplish in a speech.* Purpose is always given with an active infinitive verb—"to inform, to persuade, to motivate, to entertain, to reassure, to energize ..." followed by the specifics of this audience and situation.

I might give a speech, for instance, in which I state my purpose this way: "To excite the sales force about the changes in the company that they can communicate to our current customers."

Notice how this gives me as speaker a specific and active goal for my presentation. I can talk about the changes the company is implementing in any number of ways. But if my purpose is to actually excite my salespeople, my approach must be in a particular direction.

Note also how the purpose is entirely different from the topic, say, the recent upgrades to a software program that will make life much easier for our customer base. Those improvements are what I need to talk about *in the process of turning my listeners on.* Topic is always used as a means to accomplish our purpose as speakers. It consists of the facts, evidence, stories, reports, deliverables, experiences, and any and all other material you will include in your speech to accomplish that purpose.

Now you a) understand your audience, and b) have a specific purpose to accomplish, given that audience's make-up and needs. Let's move on to Quick Tip #9, which shows you how to efficiently organize your material into a theme that will resonate with your listeners.

9   Four Classic Formats for Organizing Your Thoughts

Remember, from Quick Tip #8: your *purpose* is what you hope to accomplish in your presentation; and your *content* is whatever you're going to say, show, or do to achieve that purpose. If you think in these terms, your content will always grow appropriately and organically out of your purpose.

But what about a theme that you can build your speech around and a logical framework that will get you there? Theme-based speeches and presentations are inherently powerful and persuasive. And when they proceed logically, listeners can stay with you every step of the way.

Here are four classic formats for organizing your speeches. Each of them, importantly, allows a solid level of audience involvement with your thinking to take place. Which of these approaches you use depends on the nature of your audience, your purpose with those listeners, and your content. Any one of those variables can change depending upon the speaking situation, and your chosen format should also change accordingly.

1. **Chronological.** Perhaps your presentation lends itself to a chronological approach. An employee talk on handling change, for instance, might take a look backward at company practices up to now then present the reasons why new procedures need to be put into place. Talks on historical subjects also lend themselves to this format.

2. **Problem-Solution.** Do your listeners need to be educated about a problem before you and they can discuss possible solutions? A problem-solution format would work well in that situation. If your audience needs a more in-depth examination, you might choose a Problem-Cause-Solution style of organization.

3. **Compare Solutions.** If on the other hand your audience is

already acquainted with the issues, you may elect to skip the discussion of the problem and go right to possible solutions. Now you can talk about the advantages and disadvantages of each approach instead of giving your listeners information they already have.

A speech on urban gang violence, for instance, might benefit from a Problem-Cause-Solution format when given to the charitable giving officers of a corporation. A group of social workers who deal with gang violence every day, on the other hand, might appreciate a more direct approach that compares solutions instead.

4. **Tell a Story.** All human beings love stories. Can you frame your presentation around a compelling story? We all have stories to tell—companies and organizations no less than individuals. If you frame your message in the context of a story, with all the drama, conflict, and emotions that people bring to their actions, you will have a *very* captive audience.

10 Using an Outline Can Help You Think

Let's talk outlines.

An outline, as your high school teacher used to tell you, is a superb tool for organizing your thoughts into a logical structure.

But outlines needn't look like the classical form of "I" followed by "A" followed by "1." and "(a)," "(1)," and so on.

At its best and simplest, an outline is merely a framework to help you get down your main points, along with evidence to support or amplify those points. And that's it. How basic or complex your outline becomes depends entirely upon your own comfort zone.

If outlining intimidates you, maybe this will help: think of the process as merely jotting down notes or getting your ideas on paper (or computer screen).

For the purposes of public speaking, two types of outline are most helpful: the Preparation Outline and the Speaking Outline. (I am indebted to Stephen E. Lucas and his book *The Art of Public Speaking* for this dichotomy.) And yes, the use of each is as straightforward as it sounds. Let's look at the features and advantages of the two forms:

Preparation Outline: This is the outline you piece together early in your work on content. It helps you corral your thoughts and place them in an order that makes sense. Worthwhile features of the preparation outline include the following points:

◆ Using full sentences helps you get your thoughts together.
◆ The logical framework of your presentation becomes much clearer.
◆ You don't have to write out your entire speech.
◆ Sections of your content are easy to move around and reorder.

Speaking Outline: When it comes time to deliver your present-ation, however, you need a more concise delivery tool. Otherwise, your listeners will end up staring at the top of your head as you read the lengthy manuscript in front of you. Instead, you should include only key words and phrases.

Your speaking outline, then, will be much shorter than your preparation outline. It's really just a skeleton compared to the fleshed-out body of a preparation outline. The speaking outline is helpful in at least three ways:

◆ It forces you to look at your audience, not your notes.
◆ It provides a "springboard" for your stories and personal connection to your topic.
◆ It allows for personal notes, e.g., "Remember eye contact,"

"Say this list slowly," etc.

When you use an outline like this, made up only of key words and phrases that function as reminders when you talk, you are speaking *extemporaneously*. The term simply means using prepared notes and practicing beforehand (as opposed to *impromptu* or "off-the-cuff" speaking).

Extemporaneous is the ideal speaking style for establishing rapport with your listeners. But by preparing a full-sentence preparation outline in your planning phase, you will have helped yourself express your ideas in fully formed, logically constructed thoughts.

11 Put Stories in Your Presentation Toolbox

Recently a Fortune 500 company hired me to coach one of their young executives for an upcoming speech. The talk would be part of a company-wide conference, and this executive was scheduled to deliver his presentation *four times* over as many days.

The executive was young, extremely bright, and since he was foreign-born, had an accent. Because his audience would consist of the top leadership of the company, his boss wanted his presentation to be as dynamic and comprehensible as possible.

My office is in Boston, and the young executive was in Cleveland. The conference would be held in Atlanta. I suggested that, if possible, the full-day coaching session should take place in the actual room where the presentation would be given. The company agreed, and flew us both to the conference center in Atlanta from different directions.

So we worked—just the two of us in a cavernous conference room—that entire day. Since this was the venue of the actual speech, we were able to use the real space as we planned how my client could look and sound as authoritative as possible. It was a luxury I know we both appreciated.

At one point, he said, "You know, my boss says you're one of the most expensive speech coaches in the country." I grinned slightly, tried to look worth the money, and kept my mouth shut.

After some further discussion, we ran through the introduction to his speech while I videotaped his performance. Then, since credibility was going to be a critical issue for this presenter, I coached him for thirty minutes on ways he could open his talk with more power and authority. Again, I taped him. Then we watched both versions.

When he saw the second take, his jaw dropped.

"Wow!" he said, when he saw his improvement. "That's incredible!"

"That's why I'm so expensive," I replied calmly (inwardly thankful that, after his earlier comment, our session was proceeding so positively!).

Do you believe at this point that, as a consultant and author, I know what I'm talking about when it comes to presentation skills? If you do, I'd venture to say it's partly because of the *story* I just told you.

I used this true story as evidence, not only to illustrate what I'm discussing in this Quick Tip, but to maintain my own credibility with you, the reader. This tool will work exactly the same way for you when you speak.

Stories provide one of the most effective approaches you'll ever find for boosting your credibility with listeners. And since the whole idea is to *influence* your audience in some way, you desperately need such authority. Stories from your own experience that resonate with listeners give you that "badge of authenticity," while making your message much clearer for your audience.

So put this essential tool in your presentation toolbox.

◆ ◆ ◆

CHAPTER

Twelve Easy Ways to Achieve Presence and Charisma

◆ ◆ ◆

"Sow a habit, and you reap a character;
Sow a character, and you reap a destiny."
— ANONYMOUS

12 True 'Inspiration': Breathing for Focus and Presence

in.spi.ra.tion

1. a breathing in, as of air into the lungs; inhaling. **2.** an inspiring or being inspired mentally or emotionally. **3.** an inspiring influence; any stimulus to creative thought or action (*Webster's New World Dictionary, Second College Edition*).

Surprised to learn that the first dictionary definition of "inspiration" has to do with *breathing?* Yet how appropriate. And how interesting that together, the definitions of this Latin word mean to take air in and then be stimulated into creativity!

In the days since those guys and gals in togas, we've mostly forgotten that first important definition of inspiration—that we need to take in oxygen not only to speak but to live. Yet every good speech coach knows that calm, focused, *well lived* presentations begin with proper breathing.

Sufficient breath support not only focuses our concentration, but slows our heart rate, as it bathes our brain cells in thought-producing oxygen. And if there's ever a time when we need a well-oxygenated brain to think on our feet, it's during a presentation.

Yet that's exactly the time when we're most nervous and apt to breathe shallowly. That is why it's so important to be familiar with good breathing habits, and to practice them when speaking in public.

Get in the habit of "belly breathing." That simply means breathing with the help of your diaphragm (the dome-shaped muscle located horizontally between lungs and abdomen) rather than with just the upper part of your lungs.

Here's how to breathe diaphragmatically or belly-breathe: Stand at ease, and place your dominant hand on your belly, i.e., at the place that goes in and out most noticeably when you breathe. That's your diaphragmatic area. Take relaxed, medium-deep breaths. Feel the bellows-like action going on down there? Breathe in = belly out.

If you stand in front of a mirror, you'll see the movement clearly. When you get in the habit of belly breathing like this, you'll be constantly giving yourself a full supply of nourishing, vital oxygen. You'll automatically become more calm and focused. And that means you'll have a much more professional and capable presence.

13 How to Look and Sound Confident

Try this simple experiment: Stand and expel all the air from your lungs until they are completely empty. What did that action do to your posture?

You probably assumed a concave and "caved in" appearance, making you appear weak and irresolute. Now, slowly fill your lungs up to their full capacity. . . .

Did that straighten you up? Do you feel more capable, prepared, and *stronger*? I bet you do—and I guarantee that's how your audience will perceive you!

You just used breathing, posture, and stance to change your level of credibility and authority with an audience. Incredible, isn't it?

Let's talk some more about how the use of space, along with time can affect your listeners' perception of you as a public speaker.

Space. What the brief exercise above accomplishes, is to allow me to introduce the concept of *controlling space*. As I stated earlier in this book, most of us become wrapped up in both our content and our nervousness when we speak in public. If we think about physical performance at all, it's to reflect how uncomfortable we are in front of all these people, and that we don't know what to do with our hands and arms.

Powerful speakers, however, go far beyond this elementary awareness of nonverbal communication. They understand how greatly physical presence affects credibility and believability.

Speakers who "command space" in this way positively influence their listeners' responses to them and their message. The more comfortable such speakers appear to be as they stand and move, the more likely audience members will identify with them. Conversely, of course, awkward speakers just make us feel awkward as well.

And when we're that uncomfortable with a speaker, we tend to resist their critically important message as well.

Good speakers, on the other hand, reach their level of comfort by occupying an appropriate amount of space. They strike a balance between diminishing their authority by folding in on themselves, and gesticulating wildly or pacing back and forth like a caged animal (what I call "the motivational speaker syndrome").

You can experiment with what it feels like to stand and move powerfully as a presenter. Pay attention to what it feels like for you physically when you're doing something familiar and enjoyable.

Commit those physical sensations to your muscle-memory. Now *recreate* them at will, as you pretend you're standing in front of an audience. With practice, you'll begin to teach your body some of these "new tricks"!

Time. Just as we want to control how we occupy space, we must keep a firm grasp on time as an element in our presentations. On the most basic level, this means keeping to our agenda, so that we don't lop off important parts of our talk because we're up against the clock.

I once coached a partner and a vice president of a consulting firm, then attended the conference the pair was speaking at. The partner (who presented first), couldn't resist going down the path of questions that took him off his topic, until the time left for his partner had evaporated completely.

In your practice sessions, get to know what 5, 20, and 40 minutes feel like in a speaking situation. And keep in mind that time is extremely *subjective* to a speaker—stretching out like salt water taffy or compressing shockingly—while remaining basically *objective* to audiences.

Learn also how to pace your presentations. Confident speakers take the time they need to cover important points; nervous speakers fly through everything too fast.

That is, practice using *pauses* and *silence*. You may think these two tools are unnecessary intrusions into your stream of speech, but just the opposite is true. Listeners need permission to take a "mental breath" now and again.

It's one of the ways you keep audience members attuned to what you're saying. A pause in vocalization also alerts your listeners that a new and important point is coming up.

14 Tap Into Your Natural Talents

Let's face it—for audiences, the message and the messenger are usually the same thing.

It's certainly the case in politics, isn't it? The same is true in a court trial. How many of us would want to be represented by a lawyer who seems to be wearing juror repellent?

What this means is that to a large extent, you are the message your audience receives.

So you'd better be aware of the impression you're broadcasting! This Quick Tip and the three that follow discuss ways you can increase your influence on audiences, by maximizing the critical connection between you and your message.

The first and perhaps most important point to be understood is that *you are a natural performer.* As sociologist Erving Goffman reminded us in his 1972 book, *The Presentation of Self in Everyday Life,* each of us plays many roles in our daily lives.

We shape ourselves, that is, to meet the needs of the particular audience we're with at the moment. The "you" shopping in the supermarket, for instance, is a different person from the "you" on a first date, or the one explaining to your boss the reasons you deserve a raise.

This knowledge, that we play different roles even in a typical day, should be a liberating thought. By acknowledging that a speech situation is simply one of the many "performances" we give every day of our lives, we can embrace each such opportunity instead of fearing it.

In other words: there really is nothing unusual or momentous about speaking in public. We're *always* giving some kind of performance or other in our lives. Public speaking just gives us the opportunity to do it all with a bit more *pizzazz!*

15 Show Audiences Your Goodwill

Do you give your audiences the impression that you're speaking for *their* benefit, not your own?

That's what "goodwill" means for a presenter—and it's a quality that's absolutely essential for speaking success.

Yet how often have you seen speakers who appear to love to listen to themselves talk? For instance, the next time you attend a meeting or presentation, pay attention to whether the speaker is making an effort to be sure his or her audience is receiving critical information.

Does he or she make eye contact? Is the speaker seeing the nonverbal communication coming his or her way (if a listener slips into a coma in a forest, does an oblivious speaker even hear it happening)? Does that person stop their soliloquy from time to time to solicit input from others in the room or auditorium?

Just eye contact, for instance, can make an enormous difference: How can anyone even pretend to be concerned with the needs of an audience if the notes on a lectern are more important than the people in the seats?

It just makes sense: audiences who think a speaker cares about them are infinitely more inclined to trust and be influenced by that presenter.

Remember, you should be in complete control as a speaker. *You* have the power to shape the thoughts and opinions of others; and in some cases, to change people's lives.

To be a responsible speaker is to use that power benignly and constructively. Playing power politics with your audiences can reap short-term benefits; yet eventually, the message of who you really are will emerge.

As a speaker, you must place your listeners front-and-center at all times. *Look* at people when you talk to them, and use facial expressions—exactly the way you would to a friend sitting across from you at Starbucks.

And pay attention to people's reactions. If they appear confused or uninterested, you may have to repeat a key item, state something a different way, or think up a metaphor to illustrate your point.

Here's a touchstone you can use when it comes to gauging your goodwill as a speaker: If you are truly and completely engaged with the needs of your listeners, you won't experience a single "How am I doing?" moment. You'll simply have more important things on your agenda.

16 Reveal Your True Self

One of the fascinating things about speaking in public is that it reveals so much about who we are as human beings. As I tell my clients and trainees: even as a former actor, I would have to work ferociously hard to hide my true nature when I talk to people about something that really matters to me.

And if I did, all of my focus and concentration would be directed *inward* instead of where it needs to be—on keeping my audience actively engaged with my critical message.

The problem with being this comfortable with self-exposure occurs when we perceive a speaking situation as something "different" and intimidating. That's when we become nervous and afraid; and in response, we slip on our presentation masks or don our invisible protective armor.

In other words—we temporarily become someone we really

aren't.

And audiences sense it immediately.

We need to throw away the mask, to let our true self come through for our sake and our listeners'.

We need, in other words, to remain vulnerable.

You may think that's too hard a task to accomplish in front of other professionals, and perhaps complete strangers. But believe me—the opposite is true. Being honest with an audience makes everything easier on both sides.

Hiding from who you really are is much harder work for you *and* your listeners.

17 Have a Dialogue With Your Listeners

A speech or presentation can easily seem like a one-way street: You send, your audience receives, and that's it.

Yet that's not how a good presentation works. In a dynamic talk or speech, information passes back and forth continuously. It's true that most of that information is verbal on your part and nonverbal on the part of your audience (except in question-and-answer sessions). Still, every presentation involves give-and-take of information and sensory input. In that sense, every good speech is more dialogue than monologue. So it stands to reason that we have to pay attention to the nonverbal communication that's coming our way as our audience's "speech."

That way, we remain flexible and *conversational* with our listeners. And people are most persuaded when someone is talking to them rather than *at* them.

At this point you might ask: "How can I possibly converse with an audience that's sitting out there in silence?" Like so many aspects of public speaking, it just takes practice. Here's a good way to achieve a conversational dynamic in your speaking ability:

In your next conversation with someone on a topic that really interests you, pay attention to how you express yourself vocally and physically. Hear how lively and animated your voice becomes? Notice how you move and use gestures and facial expressions? What about the way your volume, pitch, tone, and vocal quality change as you speak about your thoughts and feelings on this topic?

Now, consciously bring those aspects of your communication style into your practice sessions as a speaker or presenter. You may feel awkward at first, because you'll be intentionally transferring speaking behavior from one situation to another. But don't worry about that. You're simply teaching yourself to be more like your natural speaking self, not less.

Next, ask a friend to sit in as a practice audience. Ask him or her to tell you whenever you don't sound like the real you.

In this way, session by session, you'll be nudging your presentation persona toward your natural conversational style rather than an assumed style.

And the real you is the one that's unique and interesting for audiences.

18 How to Get an Audience to Trust You

*"It is feeling and force of imagination
that make us eloquent."*
QUINTILIAN

We have to be credible when we give a career-related presentation—that's a given. And being credible means acting businesslike and hard-headed, with a cut-to-the-chase style that banishes all emotion, right?

Rubbish!

When was the last time you made a critical decision about your life based solely on reason, leaving emotion out of it? Chances are you've never done that. As human beings, we make life-changing decisions emotionally—from the gut. Only afterwards do we justify our choices with rational arguments, convincing ourselves that we were wise to choose the path we did.

There are important biological reasons why we act this way.

You've heard about the "left brain/right brain" dichotomy, haven't you? The left side of the brain is the seat of logic, language, and reasoning. In the right hemisphere reside spatial awareness, creativity, emotions, and decision-making.

Did you notice just now that decisions and emotions are located in the same part of the brain? Why, then, would it make any sense to remove all emotional input when we're trying to persuade an audience?

Remember: audience members want to be influenced by you; so most of your listeners will not be actively resistant to your message. But for true influence to occur, an audience must believe in your honesty and trustworthiness. And that, of course, is an emotional response.

All of this is to say, that listeners are making decisions about us as presenters at the same time they're responding to our messages emotionally. So it makes no sense whatever to try to rid our presentations of emotion.

However professional we need our presentations to be— whether we're discussing sales figures, a scientific hypothesis, policy issues, or any other topic—we need to include an emotional component so that we reach the *hearts* as well as the minds of our audience members. People outside your field, for instance, may think that your material is as dry as dust. But your passion for your topic is usually shared by those who are listening to you.

A speech, any speech, is a presentation from a person or persons to other human beings. And that means that emotions will be part of the mix.

So rid yourself of the mistaken belief, if you hold it, that "feelings" is a dirty word where speeches and presentations are concerned. Find the emotional heart of what you're saying—the thing that gives your message life for you and your listeners.

Discover it, and let it show. If nothing else, your passion will intrigue your audience and generate respect for you as the presenter, while adding interest to your topic in listeners' minds.

19 Do This to Make a Lasting Impression

What is it about a dynamic speaker that grabs our attention and compels our interest?

Well, for one thing, such speakers possess *authority*. We may or may not recognize them as experts before the occasion of their speech. But once they begin to talk, there's something about the way they stand and move, isn't there? Such speakers know how to hold themselves and command the space around them.

In a word, they exhibit confidence. And critically, they do so in terms of *physicality*.

I believe that most speakers are confident in their message. They strongly believe they have the knowledge and ability to get that message across. The issue with presenters who need a greater level of authority isn't knowledge or commitment, then. It's finding a way to "broadcast" that level of passion—to *externalize* what they're thinking and feeling. And, conversely, to keep their nervousness from being visible.

That may sound like a daunting task, but it's really much easier than you might think.

Externalizing our deep commitment to our message, and our interest in speaking on this topic, really comes down to one thing: using nonverbal communication effectively. Audience members aren't mind readers. They can't intuit our expertise, our passion for our topic, or our concern that they understand our message. We have to show them these things. Remember, first impressions are lasting impressions. So it's critical to convince your listeners right away that they can relax, that they're in capable hands.

How can you do that?

Keep in mind, first of all, that "how you stand affects your standing with your audience." Evaluate your posture (use a mirror, a colleague, a spouse). And think about how you occupy space: do you "take" the space that's allotted to you as a speaker, or do you try to minimize your physical presence?

If posture (your "standing") is a problem for you, imagine that there's a piece of string tied to the top of your head that goes upward into infinity. Someone up there is tugging gently and steadily on the line, straightening you up in a slow continuous process. None of the *"Ten-shun!"* of a military snap to attention should be present here. Your posture should be upright but not stiff.

When it comes to movement, use gestures that are inclusive rather than exclusive (e.g., an open palm offered to a questioner rather than a pointed finger). Take a step in the direction of someone who speaks to you from the audience, or at least lean towards them.

And please, don't be afraid to come out from behind the lectern if you feel the need to do so. You are allowed to use the empty space on the stage or podium! (Incidentally, a *podium* is the platform you stand on when you speak; a *lectern* is the structure you stand behind.)

Finally, remember that just as emotions produce physical responses, the opposite is true: If you assume a confident and authoritative pose, you'll actually feel more credible and professional, and your audience will see the difference immediately.

20 What Is Your Body Saying?— Using Nonverbal Communication

Now that we've looked at the importance of holding yourself well and commanding space (Quick Tip #19), let's talk about how you can maximize your skills at "nonverbal communication." You've probably heard that term many times, and perhaps you've wondered what it refers to in terms of presentation skills.

Nonverbal communication means everything you communicate to your audience apart from the words you say. Your content (words) is a critical part of your message, of course. But studies have shown that what you *look and sound like* as you're delivering information plays a central role in the message that's received by your listeners.

In research conducted at U.C.L.A. and published in 1981, communications expert Albert Mehrabian found that *93 percent* of message reception comes from nonverbal communication over verbal content. Mehrabian was specifically focused on messages with a high emotional content. But the kernel of his findings remains: A huge proportion of your effectiveness as a presenter depends upon your appearance, movement, and vocal presentation.

A classic example of this dynamic in action is the opening debate in the Kennedy-Nixon presidential contest of 1960—the first televised presidential debate in history. Nixon at that point in the campaign was ahead in the polls. But how he *appeared* on television in that critically important first debate hurt his candidacy considerably.

Viewers had no idea that the Vice President actually had the flu that day. What they saw was a man with a hastily applied make-up job who was sweating profusely in the harsh studio lights, and generally looking ill at ease in the new medium of television.

Across from Nixon was the tanned, athletic-looking Jack Kennedy, who not only gave the impression of youthful vigor, but intuitively seemed to understand how to use the cameras to advantage.

Interestingly, post-debate polls showed that among voters who *listened* to the debate on radio, Nixon was judged the winner. But the nonverbal message that millions of television viewers received was that Nixon was not up to the sheer physical demands of the American presidency.

You're probably not running for office—but what your body and vocal instrument are telling audiences is no less critical to your success. Unfortunately, there's no magic pill I can give you to make you a more effective nonverbal communicator. But I can offer what I think is a valuable suggestion:

Spend less time on the *content* of your presentation, and more time on how you hold yourself, move, and sound as you speak. Some excellent tools to help you in this pursuit are a) a mirror, b) friends and colleagues, and most important, c) a camcorder.

With their help, you'll begin to see and hear yourself as others do. That's a crucial step in knowing how to marshal nonverbal communication to your success and profit.

21 Speaking With Credibility and Authority

Let's face it: there are times when you want to come across as warm and friendly in your presentations: a team player. Then there are other occasions when you need to project a bedrock image of absolute credibility and authority.

Achieving that second goal—a high level of perceived professionalism—is what I'd like to discuss in this tip.

If you're senior enough or your reputation precedes you,

attaining that degree of credibility is usually easy. But what about these common situations:

◆ You're young (or you sound that way).
◆ You're speaking to listeners who are more senior than you are.
◆ You're the first representative of your company (or organization, or government) these listeners have ever seen.
◆ You're female, in an industry historically populated only by men.

In these circumstances and similar situations, you're apt to lack confidence in the role you've been assigned to play. And with good reason.

Fortunately, the world of the theater offers an easy and remarkably effective exercise to help you. This is not surprising, since actors face the biggest credibility challenge of all: convincing audiences that they're someone everyone knows they're not!

The exercise is to imagine you're a tree. (Aren't you glad you paid good money for this book?)

Seriously, the reason I want you to picture yourself as a tree has to do with the very important concept of "grounding." Stage performers understand that much of their power in performance comes from the "ground" they're standing on. In the earliest forms of theater, of course, that meant the earth itself. And if the earth itself doesn't have the ability to lend you power, what does?

In the grounding exercise, we imagine that just like a 100-year-old oak or maple, we have roots that go deep and wide into the earth. Like that tree, we are firm, secure, and unshakeable as we stand tall and proud.

Now, what do you think an audience member *sees* when he or she contemplates you as a speaker? A figure of standing and substance: a strong and steadfast presenter. If an opponent happens to send a lightning bolt your way in the question-and-answer period, you'll be strong enough to take the blast and still be standing when the smoke clears.

Speakers who lean on one hip or cross their ankles behind a lectern, on the other hand, have a hard time convincing us that they're a figure of authority. Try it yourself: Stand with your feet set solidly at armpit-width, and then with your legs crossed at the ankles. Which position makes you feel stronger and more professional?

When we plant ourselves firmly in front of others, the self-image that's elicited in our minds is that of a confident and pre-pared speaker. From that thought emerge other *physical expressions* of our confidence. It's a self-regulating cycle that continually gives us what we might call "strength of character" as a presenter.

Combine this deep-rooted sense of presence with the diaphragmatic breathing I discussed in Quick Tip #12. Now you'll look *and* sound like a person of consequence—and credi-bility and authority will flow your way.

22 How to Make Yourself a Powerful Speaker

It's a lot easier to make yourself a powerful speaker than you might imagine.

And power—in terms of the dynamism of your platform skills—matters greatly in the world of business speeches and pre-sentations.

You may be the world's foremost authority on your subject. Yet the inescapable fact concerning presentations, is that you will be measured as much on your *performance* as your knowledge or expertise.

Political consultant Roger Ailes understood the juncture of self and message well, when he titled his 1988 public speaking book *You Are the Message.*

In plain terms, your audiences will equate your message with *you.* And that's a good thing. Otherwise, you could send out a blast e-mail of your speech, and no one would have to show up—including you.

So from today on, think in terms of the "speaking version" of you—a performance persona that's the essence of you talking about your subject area. That's the person your audiences will find interesting.

In other words, it's not enough just to be who you are when you present. You have to construct a performance version of yourself. That requires marrying your honesty and truthfulness about your message, to some simple but powerful presentation skills.

Here are three areas of speech performance to keep in mind in this regard:

1. **Competence.** Advertise your competence in everything you say and do. When you trust yourself and what you are saying, your audience will trust you. That's the first step that allows them to invest you with presence and authority.

   Every audience, that is, wants to feel that they're in good hands. Make it easy for listeners to relax and trust that you are such a speaker. All it takes to start is for you to trust *yourself.*

   Notice that I have used the word "trust" four times in these two short paragraphs. This is not a subtle hint.

2. **Rapport.** Find a way to identify with your audience's values and experiences, and externalize the connection by what you say. Most listeners resist speakers whose background or known views are noticeably different from their own. Wherever you can, show that you and your listeners share common ground. Remember that our experiences, motivations and feelings unite all of us around the world far more than they divide us. Create an atmosphere in your presentations that fosters persuasion and believability.

And remember to be interesting! You can judge this yourself in your practice sessions. If you're looking forward to just getting this painful experience over with, your audience will, too.

3. **Delivery.** Every audience arrives with preconceptions about a speaker. These may have nothing to do with you personally, but be tied to the topic, organization, or viewpoint you represent.

You need to show that you are able to "deliver" on the implied promise that your presentation has created, i.e., that it will be worth spending time and effort to listen to. That's what *delivery* means in this respect. When you give your speech dynamically and with conviction, you'll be "delivering" the goods!

Credibility resides in speakers who appear confident and committed. And of course, there's simply no substitute for enthusiasm. Embody your arguments with an energetic delivery, and you'll go a long way toward changing the thinking and behavior of your audience.

23 Your Best Visual Aid Is . . . You!

Remember Bill Clinton?

Whether you favor Che Guevara T-shirts, or quote William F. Buckley at cocktail parties, you'll probably agree with me that William Jefferson Clinton was and is a charismatic public speaker.

What made President Clinton so good at the lectern? Certainly, he was smooth. And he displayed an extraordinary sense of ease, coupled with firm control. Not many speakers, after all, could deliver a nationally televised address from memory while a TelePrompTer relentlessly rolled out the wrong speech!

Perhaps Clinton's chief attribute as a speaker, however, was the pure enjoyment he displayed speaking to audiences.

But let's step back a moment, and ask ourselves how we know that. How is it possible that we can reasonably guess Clinton's feelings about speaking in public, since we're not mind-readers?

Well, it was obvious *visually,* wasn't it? The body language, the easy stance and gestures, the frequent smiles, and the sheer joy of performing. All of these things declared that this was a man who lived for these moments in his professional life.

Bill Clinton, then, is an excellent example of an important phenomenon in public speaking, one that most speakers aren't aware of: *you yourself are always your best visual aid.*

We've already seen, in Tip #20 on nonverbal communication, that visual input has a huge (55% or so) impact on how audiences receive your messages. And you're probably already sufficiently focused on the charts, graphs, PowerPoint, and handouts you routinely use as visual tools.

But your most important visual persuader isn't any of these *accoutrements.* It's you.

Think about it for a moment: You are the one visual component of your speech that's always on stage front and center. You are the visual that doesn't just sit there, but walks and talks and argues convincingly—the one that shares the beliefs of audience members and speaks to them from common ground. You're also the only visual that can adapt as need be, thinking on your feet and changing your presentation in response to audience input.

All very powerful stuff.

So don't relinquish your power as a visual persuader to your "visual aids." Your audience has seen endless charts and PowerPoint slides and workbooks. But they have either never seen you, or they haven't seen you talking about this topic *today.*

Spend the time you think is necessary to put together the visual components of your presentation. These elements are still excellent forms of evidence. Learn the techniques of working with your visual aids, and practice going through your

PowerPoint show.

But *before* you do all that—give some serious thought to how you'll look and move in front of your audience as you make your compelling arguments. The visual element of your speech that is "you," is a hugely important persuader. Find ways to make it work to your advantage.

CHAPTER

The Power of Your Voice

Invent the phrase at the very moment it is uttered.
— JOHN BARTON

24 The 5 Essential Vocal Tools

Let's assume that a Vocal Godmother has just offered you 5 magic tools that will keep your audiences attentive, engaged, and thoroughly informed and persuaded concerning your topic.

Your voice, in other words, will now *turn people on* to what you're saying.

You agree on the spot, of course. As you sit eagerly with ears poised, your vocal savior opens her magic toolbox. These are the five gifts she hands you, one by one—reminding you that they should be used *together* for greatest effect:

1. **Emphasis**
2. **Pitch Inflection**

3. **Variety in Rhythm and Pacing**
4. **Pauses and Silence**
5. **Vocal Quality**

She explains each gift to you in turn:

"Emphasis," my dear, [she says] "is simply the force or stress you place on important ideas, concepts, or feelings. It's the simplest of the tools, and I'm sure you already use it instinctively.

"Pitch inflection. As you probably already know, my pet, 'pitch' refers to where your voice is placed on the musical scale. Lively pitch inflection helps you avoid monotony and also convey meaning. A wonderful tool indeed!

"If you find, for instance, that your voice has a 'flat' quality without many variations in pitch, it's a good possibility that self-consciousness about speaking in public is inhibiting your expression.

"But you don't have this problem sitting around chatting with friends, do you? To strengthen your pitch inflection, then, find yourself a children's book, and read it aloud to a 3-year-old. Borrow one of the dears if need me. Tape yourself as you speak, and then listen back.

"You see how flexible your pitch can be? Now, having heard the result, you should feel more confident about using a more varied vocal pitch in your presentations... even to BIG people!

"Rhythm and Pacing. You mustn't ever be neglectful enough to let the rhythm and pace of your speech stay the same throughout. Instead, you need to vary things a bit.

"Variations in rhythm and pace aren't to be added artificially, however. They should emerge naturally from changes in the ideas, meaning, and emotions of what you're saying. If you're completely *focused* on your subject matter, this will happen.

"Let me repeat: changes in rhythm should not be imposed on your presentation, as in 'I'll speak more slowly here, and this is where I'll speed up,' etc. Instead, give your full attention to your message and how it is being received, and you'll sound good as you speak it.

"**Using Pauses and Silence.** Here we have the most neglected of the essential vocal tools! Pauses, of course, will help you achieve impact, add emphasis, build suspense, bridge ideas, 'comment' on what you've said, and accomplish many other things that will help make sense of your text. Pauses also convey relaxation and confidence in a speaker.

"You should pause *after* an important word or phrase so it will be strengthened in your listeners' minds. Pauses also help sense, since related ideas are naturally grouped together when we speak, and we instinctively pause when we're going on to something new.

"**Vocal quality** concerns the tone, richness, pleasantness, and emotional connection that you achieve through your speaking. It's the culminating effect of the other four tools! Use these tools wisely, and you'll sound connected and interested in your topic *and* your listeners."

25 Developing a Warmer, More Pleasant Sounding Voice

As speakers, it is our job to get critical information or viewpoints across to listeners, and to be audible doing it. Apart from that, why should we be concerned about the quality of our voice?

We should be very concerned, since *our voice is the most flexible instrument we own for persuading and influencing others.*

The human voice, in fact, is a supple agent of intention and subtlety of expression. Nothing else in our presentation toolbox equals it, except, perhaps, the visual impression you convey. Where visual clues are absent (in phone calls, for instance), the voice reigns supreme.

As we've already seen in earlier parts of this book, the way we look and sound *together* bestows maximum credibility and believability concerning ourselves and our message.

So let's look at how we can fine-tune our marvelous vocal instrument.

If your voice sounds harsh to you or otherwise counterproductive to your speaking goals, you should start at the most basic level of improvement, i.e., with the *breath*.

The best method for achieving fullness of sound in public speaking involves diaphragmatic or belly breathing (see also Quick Tip #12, "Breathing for Focus and Presence").

Breathing diaphragmatically not only produces sufficient energy for a strong vocal presence; it also provides a "cushion" of air that softens the voice. The combination results in a speaker who sounds calm and confident.

Shallow breathing, on the other hand, lends to the voice a thin and somewhat harsh quality, and can also give the impression that we're "hurried and harried." An average American speaks 150-180 words per minute. If you're racing along due to shallow breathing, however, you can easily exceed that range and make your listeners feel exhausted.

The second essential point regarding attaining a pleasant and warm voice has to do with anatomy. For, not surprisingly, our voice reflects what is going on in the rest of our body.

If we are frazzled and tense, our body reacts with both visible and audible responses. Just as we can see that someone is not calm and centered emotionally, for example, we can *hear* it in his or her voice.

Speaker A may be shuffling with her notes under the lectern, coming in and out of appropriate distance from the microphone, and allowing her breathing to reflect her disordered physical state, which in turn gives her voice the tinge of distance and distractedness.

Speaker B is focused on her message and her listeners, and so physically demonstrates a quality of being fully "in the present." Her voice is poised to respond to the needs of her listeners concerning her topic, and emerges as solid, steady, and strong.

Which speaker would you rather listen to?

26 ◆ Finding the Pitch That's Right for You

We often speak about the "pitch" of someone's voice. But what exactly does that mean?

As Quick Tip #24 mentioned, pitch refers to the placement of the voice on the musical scale: its highness or lowness. A voice with an extremely low pitch, such as Henry Kissinger's, has a *basso profundo* quality to it. Comedian Pee Wee Herman's voice, on the other hand, seems as light and wind-blown as a feather.

As a speaking professional, you should know about two aspects of this important vocal tool: *habitual pitch* and *optimal pitch*. The vocal pitch we use out of habit, that is, may not be the one best suited for our physiology and vocal health: our "optimal" pitch.

Males and females not only have differences in vocal anatomy, but they often respond differently in terms of habitual vs. optimal pitch. Men have a tendency to sit on their pitch, forcing it down into their lowest registers, where they believe they sound most masculine and authoritative. Women, however, sometimes head in the opposite direction, lightening their voice artificially to sound sweet and girlish.

You may not take either approach, and of course you shouldn't. But too many of us *are* guilty of using an undifferentiated pitch that gives our speech an uninflected and monotonous quality.

In any case, it's worth knowing whether the pitch you're using is right for you in terms of vocal health and quality of sound production. Here are two quick-and-easy ways to find out:

Method #1: Without thinking about it beforehand, record yourself singing "Happy Birthday." (I once coached a member of the U.S. House of Representatives who thought this suggestion was slightly mad. Fortunately, I didn't respond concerning anything that takes place under the dome of the U.S. Capitol.)

Once you've sung "Happy Birthday," say something into the tape recorder in what you consider your normal pitch. The two recordings—the song and the spoken passage—should match fairly closely. If they don't, "Happy Birthday" is closer to your optimal pitch because it was spontaneous.

Method #2: Sing a sustained note somewhere in the middle of your vocal range. Now "step down" one note on the musical scale at a time, i.e., "Do," "Ti," "La," "So," and so on. Continue until you reach the lowest note you can *sustain* without your voice breaking up. Now, come *up* two or three notes on the scale. That's your optimal pitch.

If you've just found that your habitual pitch (the one you're used to using) doesn't match your optimal pitch (your healthiest and most effective pitch), make any necessary adjustments. Now try using what you know is your optimal pitch.

Don't be discouraged if it takes time for you to get used to your new pitch. You may have been using this not-so-good-for-you pitch for years. After all, that's one of the definitions of a habit, isn't it? With time and a bit of concentration, though, you'll develop a new and more beneficial vocal habit.

You might say it's as easy as Do-Re-Me!

27 Are You Singing Your Speech or Just Mouthing the Words?

Did you ever consider that delivering an outstanding presentation is like performing a great song? Not only is the "music" delightful to listen to, but your voice soars on a combination of dynamic technique and an inspirational message. The way you use your vocal tools, that is, carries astonishing weight with regard to credibility, authority, and that all-important attribute, believability.

Why does your voice alone make such a difference? Well, for one thing, we all respond in basic and even primitive ways to the qualities of a person's voice. If a voice is pleasant and authoritative, for instance, it inspires confidence in the listener. But a voice that comes across as unpleasant, weak or too timid nudges that same listener in the opposite direction.

Vocal dynamics, or vocal variety, is one of the most powerful tools presenters possess to win over audiences. The elements of vocal dynamics—tone quality, pitch placement, inflection, use of emphasis, variations in pace and tempo, employing pauses, and all the emotional nuances our voices can project—offer us a nearly limitless palette to "paint word pictures" and convince others. When we employ vocal dynamics as we speak, we make our stories and ideas come vibrantly alive for our listeners.

The potential of your voice. One effective way to realize your vocal potential is simply to keep in mind that the voice is inherently physical. That fact may sound obvious, but it's easy to forget when one is preoccupied with the content of a presentation.

Your voice is intimately connected to breathing, energy, and relaxation. It also reflects tension and stress. That means that the pressures of a too-hectic lifestyle (or professional schedule) will emerge in one form or another in your vocal expression. Anything you can do to relieve those pressures—yoga, sports, relaxation exercises—will pay off in a more fluid and powerful vocal instrument.

Getting to flow. To be convincing as a speaker, you must combine the use of your voice with what you are saying. Beautiful words that don't sound meaningful will not convince people; but neither will the passionate delivery of a package empty of ideas.

Content's ultimate power and effectiveness hinges on your ability to combine the quality of your voice and your nonverbal communication. The key here is *commitment*. When you fully commit to your message and your passionate need to convey it to listeners, your vocal presentation will achieve a natural flow, which aids persuasion.

Delivering honesty. Once you're aware of your potential for vocal power, you can learn how to more subtly influence your audience. The suppleness of the vocal instrument is a factor presenters too often ignore.

The voice is the perfect tool to build trust; to instill confidence in a product, service, or idea; to create excitement among auditors; and to achieve many other positive outcomes. But for this level of change to occur in audience members, they must trust and respect you as a speaker. That means you must have an honest conversation with them, rather than "speechifying," or manipulating your message or listeners.

There are no tricks to influencing audiences. It all comes down—first, foremost, and finally—to honesty.

28 ▸ Like, Eliminating "uh's," "um's," and Other Vocal Fillers

Do you think you use the non-words "uh" and "um" too much in your speech?

Chances are, you don't.

These two non-fluencies—along with "like," "okay," "right," and even "so"—are examples of what communication experts call *vocal fillers* or *vocalized pauses*. Whatever you call them, they can be as annoying for speakers as for listeners.

But vocal fillers are hardly the biggest problem you'll face as a presenter. And anyway, the perception of the problem is usually worse than the reality. We tend to focus on these minor verbal tics the way we worry about the size of our ears or our nose. In other words, we give them greater importance than they usually deserve.

The other danger with regard to vocalized pauses is that, somewhere along the line, someone mentioned that you say "uh" too much. From then on, every time you give a speech, all you hear is yourself saying "Uh" for what seems like a thousand times, as the entire rest of your speech disappears in your own mind.

Believe me, this is not what your audience is focusing on! They are there to hear you say something of interest or importance to them, and getting that message across is what you should be focusing on.

But if you insist on ridding your speech of vocal fillers, here are three ways you can do it:

1. **Discover the beauty of the pause.** Pauses in public speeches are lovely things. Used sparingly and wisely, pauses are powerful vocal tools that allow listeners to reflect on the important point just made. They also aid our speeches by

helping to vary our pacing. A presentation without pauses is like a 100-car freight train going by at a railroad crossing: endless and boring. Listeners need a mental rest now and then. Pauses accomplish that.

Speakers who pause also sound confident, since they're obviously not rushing to get the whole painful ordeal over with. Even better, pauses in a lengthy presentation are as refreshing as a sip of cool water on a sweltering day.

2. **Work with a tape recorder or video camera.** With any unproductive habit, first becoming aware of the problem is the critical step. So you may want to find out whether your vocal filler problem is as pronounced as you think it is.

If you find that that is the case, practice speaking into a tape recorder and then listening to yourself. At this stage, you'll hear practically nothing *but* your vocalized pauses. But give it time, and remember that it's not as bad as it sounds— you're only super-focused on the issue at the moment. Gradually, you'll improve. It's not a quick-fix, but there really is no fast solution to this ingrained vocal practice.

3. **Enlist the help of a friend.** Have a friendly practice session in which a friend or colleague helps you with the problem. The person should listen to you speak while giving an auditory cue each time you use your favorite vocal filler—tapping on the table, ringing a small bell, that sort of thing.

Each time you hear the cue you must stop and start that sentence over. Personally, I would try the first two options before undertaking this one, because you might find it too frustrating. And for goodness sake, don't choose a member of your family to do this with!

29   Is Your Voice Helping or Hurting You?

It's pretty obvious that *what* you say in a presentation matters more than the *way* you say it.

Right?

If you believe that, try reading the following short passages aloud. Speak them first in a flat monotone, then with expression, as if this is the most important thing you'll say all year:

◆ "You may have heard that this company is washed up . . . finished. But I'm here to tell you: Acme Industries is going to win back our share of the industry. And you're the only people who can make that happen!"

◆ "The United States is absolutely committed to preventing further genocide—in this region or anywhere in the world."

◆ "I love you."

Did you find any differences in *underlying meaning* as you spoke neutrally or with emotion?

Now try reading aloud the short sentence below. Emphasize only one word each time, starting with the first word and moving down the line (you'll be speaking aloud six sentences):

"I didn't give them those documents."

You've just conveyed *six different* messages, haven't you?

The first exercise makes use of emotional coloration in speech, the second, using emphasis for meaning. I included them both to demonstrate a critically important point in public speaking:

Nothing gives you more opportunities to persuade listeners than the way you use your voice.

No other presentation technique is capable of such infinite variety. And nothing else you say or do can achieve such subtle shades of meaning and intention. Haven't you experienced that in the way the important things in your life were expressed, by you and others?

Invest some time to discover how effectively, or not, you use your voice. In other words: come to terms with your abilities. Record yourself and listen to the sounds and intentions embodied in your voice. Try to grasp how others hear you and make decisions about you based on your voice. Then start working to improve your problem areas.

When you give presentations, include in your evaluation instrument questions that deal specifically with speech and voice issues. And try to locate a first-class speech coach, preferably someone with a background in theater or broadcasting.

Discover what your listeners already know about how your voice is helping or hurting your effectiveness as a communicator.

30 ◆ The 2-Minute Speech Warm-Up

The Quick Tips in this chapter have been concerned with developing a flexible vocal instrument—a key skill for presenters. The voice, far more than any presentation asset we possess, is a *responsive* tool, one that only awaits our skill in using it.

Once we understand the profound ways in which our voice can affect listeners, we can use our instrument to elicit a wide range of colorations and effects. We can sound somber or lighthearted; cajoling or compelling; skeptical or inspirational. Having grasped the concept of *vocal intentions,* we employ our vocal range and virtuosity to support and amplify our critical messages.

But as I've said earlier in this book, our voice is, simply and profoundly, a physical mechanism. And like any other muscle group, it needs to be warmed up to function at peak performance.

Yet given today's hectic work and travel schedules (not to mention unrealistic presentation deadlines), keeping such a workout brief is paramount.

Here, then, is a vocal warm-up that takes just two minutes. It covers three essential areas, and should be practiced in this order:

1. **Breathing and resonance;**
2. **Supporting the sound; and**
3. **Warming up the articulators.**

Breathing and Resonance

◆ Close your eyes while standing. Take 3 slow, deep breaths. Imagine breath as both nourishment and relaxing energy.

◆ Focus on your abdominal area. Feel your abdomen come outward when you breathe in, and go in when you breathe out. This is healthy controlled breathing. It is diaphragmatic or *natural* breathing.

Supported and Sustained Sound

◆ Now, breathing through the mouth, breathe in slowly to a silent count of five. Hold your breath to a silent count of five; then exhale to a silent count of five. Do this three times.

◆ Choosing a comfortable pitch, produce the sustained sound "ahh" quietly and gently, without attacking the vowel sound.

Warming Up the Articulators

◆ Next, using your fingers, manipulate your facial muscles as if they were made of rubber. Practice chewing a huge imaginary wad of bubble gum with your lips closed but your teeth apart. (Blowing imaginary bubbles is optional.)

◆ Stick your tongue out and rotate it in as wide a circle as possible (you might want to wait until your boss has left the area). Blow your lips outward in a floppy "horsey" sound.

Now speak with exaggerated articulation any sentences you like. Really allow your lips and jaw to move as much as possible. Repeat your sentence(s) two more times with this exaggerated diction.

You're all set!

You're a) breathing diaphragmatically, b) controlling and sustaining the sound, and c) speaking crisply and with good articulation.

Knock 'em dead!

CHAPTER

Dynamic Introductions and Conclusions

◆ ◆ ◆

*"Early impressions are hard to eradicate from the mind.
When once wool has been dyed purple, who can restore it to its
previous whiteness?"*
— ST. JEROME

31 **How to Grab an Audience**

Do you have key information that listeners should retain once your presentation is over?

If so, you should become acquainted with the concepts of *primacy* and *recency*. "Primacy" states that people remember most vividly what they hear at the beginning of a speech; and "recency" makes the same claim for the end. In terms of public speaking, this translates into Introductions and Conclusions.

This tip discusses your opening gambit: your Introduction.

Here are three reasons why your Introduction needs to be

engaging and interesting *immediately:*

1. Audiences make value judgments about you, your organization, and your message in the first 30-60 seconds of your presentation. After this point, you'll be able to change those opinions about as easily as you can change a hamster into a ham sandwich.
2. Your opening sets the entire tone of your presentation.
3. The first minute is when you introduce your message and tell the audience why they need to hear it.

So, some critical awareness has to be created in your audience. But that's not going to happen unless you can *grab your listeners' attention* strongly enough that they tune in to your verbal and vocal magic! Achieving this objective always takes some thought, and often, a bit of creativity.

Primacy won't have much of a chance to operate, for instance, if you use the dreary: "Today, I would like to talk about ..." approach in your opening. This is a dreadfully boring way to begin, and I invite you to throw it out of your public speaking toolbox permanently. There must be *some* appropriate-yet-intriguing ways for you to lead into your topics!

Just remember to avoid introducing your Introduction, thus: "Let me start out with a story—" or, "I heard a very funny joke the other day—" Just *tell* us the story, the joke, the in-the-know reference that will crack these audience members up. By signaling it beforehand, you water its potency down to the drizzle point.

As an aid to your own creativity regarding your opening, here are a dozen "springboard" devices that can be used as grabbers:

◆ A rhetorical or actual question
◆ An appropriate and vivid quotation
◆ Charts, graphs, or other striking visual images

◆ A relevant statistic
◆ A startling statement
◆ A personal anecdote or experience
◆ Humor
◆ A story
◆ Expert opinion on the topic at hand
◆ A sound effect or musical cue
◆ A physical object
◆ A testimonial or success story

The best grabbers engage an audience immediately, both intellectually and emotionally. Coming up with one is work—but the rewards if you're successful always justify the effort.

32 Don't Be Afraid to Advertise Your Expertise

Do you know about the Amazonian tree frogs that are poisonous to predators?

"Ah," you may be saying to yourself: "But isn't it a tad late to get that message across while you're being eaten?"

The solution, my friend, is advertising.

Those particular tree frogs are vivid yellow-and-black or orange-and-black in appearance—easy to recognize on the instant. Hungry predators spot them and think: "Nope. Not *that* one!"

Let's assume for a moment that you've read and followed the advice in the previous Quick Tip, i.e., you've grabbed your audience's attention and interest with your opener. Next, you must reveal your topic and relate it to your audience in some way. (This should be self-evident but evidently isn't, since audiences are sometimes left wondering five minutes into a presentation what the speech is all about.)

Now that you have your audience's interest, and your listeners are clear on what you're here to discuss, it's time to *advertise your competence or expertise to talk on this subject.*

The reason is that all audiences ask themselves a simple question: "Why should we listen to this person talk about this topic? What particular knowledge or experience does he or she have?"

Your influence will depend, in considerable part, on whether that question is answered positively. To avoid any fatal resistance to you and your message, then, you must let your audience know that you do in fact have authority to speak on this topic.

The things you can mention in this regard include your current job, your educational background, your years of experience, recognition you've received in this field, personal experiences—or even the fact that you have a passionate interest in this subject.

Simply make this part of your presentation brief and to the point, and find a way to fold it into the topic as it relates to this audience. Often there's a fine line between establishing your credibility and sounding egotistical.

Another solution is to let the person who introduces you help establish your credentials by listing your degrees and accomplishments, etc.

At any rate, don't let modesty make you neglect to establish your credentials. Remember those tree frogs, and how it pays to advertise.

33 Getting Your Listeners to Retain Key Information

Here are some sobering findings. Together, they remind us that we have to work hard as presenters to get listeners to retain what we say:

◆ Audience members listen with a low level of efficiency. They need to be told things three times, since they *distort* 40-60 percent of what they hear.[1]

◆ Based on research by Michael Aun, an audience's retention is strongly tied to the use of visual aids. Following a speech given with no visual reinforcement, for instance, listeners retain only about 10 percent of information. If visuals such as slides, charts, props, etc., are used, retention rises to 60 percent. And if a handout is included, the amount of information retained leaps up to 85 percent.[2]

◆ Audiences are easily bogged down by too much information. One or two key points can be managed well enough by the average listener. But once we've introduced, say, five major thoughts, our listener is juggling no less than *120 different ways* of relating the different bits of information![3]

The lesson we should take away from these findings is clear:

Our best bet for getting listeners to retain information is to offer *one major idea,* supported by evidence. This theme should be stated more than once in one form or another, including visual reinforcement.

Obviously, to make things easiest on our audience, we should begin this process at the start of our presentation, and pay attention to it at the end of our speech as well. Remember Quick Tip #31, and the concepts of *primacy* and *recency?*

That tip reminded us that, when it comes to the memorable

[1] Claudyne Wilder, *The Presentations Kit* (New York: John Wiley & Sons, 1994), vii.

[2] Jeff Slutsky and Michael Aun, *The Toastmasters International Guide to Successful Speaking* (Chicago: Dearborn Financial Publishing, 1997), 77.

[3] Stephen C. Rafe, *How to Be Prepared to Think on Your Feet* (New York: Harper Business, 1990), quoted in Lilly Walters, *Secrets of Successful Speakers* (New York: McGraw Hill, 1993), 59.

aspects of a presentation, listeners recall best what comes first and last. By combining that knowledge with the advice in this Quick Tip about how audiences retain information, we have the best chance of making an impact on the hearts and minds of our listeners.

34 Bravo! Ending Dramatically and Memorably

In Quick Tip #31, I discussed the concept of primacy: the theory that audiences retain that part of your message they hear first. The corollary is true as well: *recency* states that listeners remember in particular the last thing you said.

"Quit while you're ahead," and "Always leave them laughing," are two well-known sayings that embody this principle.

Now, think about the Conclusions to all the speeches and presentations you've listened to over the past year. How many of them were memorable? How many of them even *had* a conclusion?

One of the most common public speaking shortcomings is the lack of a memorable Conclusion that drives home one's message. For audience members, this can feel like being on the receiving end of a shaggy dog story. Or to put it another way: a speech without a conclusion leaves listeners hungry for a last satisfying mouthful of your presentation's key ingredient.

Why would you want to leave your audience without dessert?

Just as you grabbed listeners' attention at the start of your speech, you must ensure that your Conclusion is memorable and vividly re-focuses your auditor on your core message.

As with your Introduction, a solid Conclusion takes thought and sometimes a dash of creativity. You can use the very same list of a dozen "springboard" devices mentioned in Quick Tip #31 to conclude your speech as well as open it. The idea is to be sufficiently dramatic, provocative, or humorous so that your message will stick in the listener's mind afterwards.

A witticism from Oscar Wilde or Mark Twain, or a quotation from Mother Teresa or Mahatma Gandhi, can do wonders. I also suggest looking outside your narrow field of expertise to find a connection that's unexpected by your listeners and therefore invigorating.

For as Yogi Berra said: "It ain't over till it's over."

CHAPTER 6

Delivering Your Critical Messages

◆ ◆ ◆

"In uplifting, get underneath."
— GEORGE ADE

35 **How to Inspire Your Listeners**

If your message is a critical one, your presentation has to be memorable.

It's as simple and as challenging as that.

Yet how many of us business executives, salespeople, social service providers, lecturers, butchers-bakers-and-candlestick-makers meet that essential requirement?

Instead, the pitiful truth is that *most speeches and presentations are exactly like all the others in that field.* Speakers feel safe that way. Unfortunately, such presentations condemn audiences to Presentation Purgatory—that zone of free-floating anxiety where PowerPoint is the preferred instrument of torture and time stretches on to the crack of doom.

Don't take your listeners there, my friend.

If you have an important message (and if you don't, why are you giving this presentation?), you must find a way to make your critical points stick in the minds of your listeners.

Another way to say this is: For your ideas to stand out, *you* must stand out. Don't be afraid to make a splash, to be different! As a start, take a look at the five suggestions below. (And feel free to come up with your own approaches along these lines):

◆ Think about how this topic has been dealt with in the past. Why did previous speakers handle it that way? What particular advantage or disadvantage did those approaches have? Can you try something different instead?

◆ Try "suspending your expertise" in your business or field of knowledge. Imagine that you're new to all of it, i.e., look at the problem from a neophyte's point of view. Issues which were too close and familiar for you to see clearly may come sharply into focus for the first time.

◆ Come up with some *interactive exercises* for your listeners during your talk. To many audience members, this will be a revolutionary concept. So, revolt!

◆ How can you "shake up" your audience's notion that they can be passive observers? Make it clear that passivity will not be allowed during your presentations! Ask questions, and expect answers.

◆ Consider every obstacle—technological, physical, or emotional—that usually comes between speaker and listeners in this type of talk. (A lectern, seating arrangements, and failure to establish common ground are some of the usual suspects.) What can you either eliminate or include for the first time?

You certainly won't want to do all (or even any) of this in every one of your presentations. But once in a while, take a different road. Whatever happens, it should be an interesting journey for all concerned.

36 How to Persuade an Audience

Every speech or presentation is persuasive to some degree.

If you're trying to get listeners to accept your point of view—however you're going about it—you first have to persuade them that you're worth listening to. This is true no matter how dry or technical you think your material is, even with what we normally think of as strictly "informative" speaking.

A common misconception, in fact, is that it's dangerous to bring **E-M-O-T-I-O-N** into a talk about serious empirical stuff.

To which I say: *Balderdash!*

When human beings talk to other human beings, emotion is present. It may be overt, as in a motivational seminar; or it may be subtle, as in a scientific symposium. But passion is still there—for isn't passion for that topic the reason people are attending? If someone shares your commitment to a subject, a field of endeavor, or a mission, that's an emotional response.

So, let's accept the proposition that we're always persuading when we give a presentation. The degree of persuasion and the subtlety or lack of it will differ; but the need to persuade remains.

Stephen Lucas, in his book *The Art of Public Speaking,* discusses four specific types of persuasive speaking. I've adapted that idea into what I call the **C.U.R.E. Method of Persuasion.** You can think of it as a way to "cure" an audience's resistance to the message you think they need to hear. It involves the following four variables:

Credibility: Credibility must be established early in order for your listeners to accept that you are worth listening to and believing. "Perceived credibility" (in which you're recognized beforehand as an expert in this area) can help enormously. But you still need to look for ways early in your speech to mention your bona fides, your years of experience, or your sheer joy concerning speaking on this topic.

Using Evidence: Your opinion may be exquisitely considered and of the best pedigree; but as far as an audience is concerned, it's still just your opinion. What evidence can you show to back it up?

Use statistics, reports, testimony and expert opinions, stories, personal anecdotes, visuals, and anything else you think is relevant. Pay particular attention to what this audience would find convincing. Make your assertion, back it up with evidence then tell your listeners the point you are trying to make. Don't assume they'll get it, because some of them won't.

Reasoning: Audiences accept arguments that they find logical and well reasoned. Your speech or presentation therefore needs a logical framework, so listeners can understand how you reached your conclusion.

If your reasoning is sound, your audience will be with you every step of the way—and most important, they will arrive at your persuasive point the same time you do. Wonderful!

And by all means, take the time to familiarize yourself with *fallacies,* or errors in reasoning. Advertising and politics are the ideal places to understand how a fallacy plays with and twists the truth. Avoid this easy but dishonorable path to persuasion.

Emotion: As I stated above, emotion is a critical component of persuasion. Too often people shy away from emotion in public speaking, for no good reason. You should consciously use ethical emotional arguments to convince your listeners, because otherwise you're leaving the human condition out of the equation.

First, understand the mood or emotional climate in which your speech is taking place. There may be reasons, for instance, why this *particular* audience—the same one you've spoken to a dozen times in the past—may be experiencing a strong emotional reaction on this occasion.

Second, bring emotional language into your talk. Human beings make decisions emotionally then justify those decisions with a rational argument. Go for the instinctual reaction, the in-the-gut agreement, for often that is the truer one.

As far as emotional persuasion goes, remember that you are there to legitimately persuade rather than manipulate. Keep that in mind, and you'll be both ethical and effective.

37 ⬥ How to Prepare a Speech in 15 Minutes

"Barstow!" your boss bellows as you pass his office. "Sonia just called. She's stuck in Patagonia—something about a melting glacier. You'll have to make the presentation this afternoon to the Mucky-Muck Committee.... Two o'clock. Don't be late!"

"But I haven't been working on that project," you plead. "I don't know what she's planning to talk about."

"Get off your knees, Barstow. It's 1:40 now—you've got twenty minutes. Make it good!"

Twenty minutes?

You have just climbed into the Speech Pressure Cooker. In fifteen minutes, at 1:55 p.m., you will emerge from the cooker (redder in the face, no doubt), and hurry to greet the members of the Mucky-Muck Committee in the Jumper's Memorial Rooftop Terrace and Conference Room.

1:41... 1:42...

If you find yourself in a situation like this, don't despair. Assuming you have some vague knowledge of your topic, here's a quick-fix tool that can be a life-saver in such high-pressure situations. It will have you delivering a coherent, logical, and dynamic presentation in no time flat. Just follow these helpful steps:

◆ **Analyze your audience (2-4 minutes).** Who are they and what do they *need* and *want* to hear? (One of these factors may be more important than the others in this particular situation.)

◆ **Decide on your central idea (5 minutes).** What one thing do you want them to take away from this presentation—your critical message? Make it concrete and memorable!

◆ **Choose *one* organizing format from the list below and use it to put your speech together (6-8 minutes).** These are ready-made to serve your purpose efficiently and effectively:

1. **Position—Evidence—Show it in Action.** State your position, and then back it up with evidence (any type that's appropriate for this audience). Give an example(s) of that evidence, i.e., show it working. Then restate your position strongly.

2. **Chronological.** Tell your story in a past-present-(and perhaps)-future form. This simple structure can make things crystal clear and be highly effective with certain messages.

3. **Problem—Solution.** This structure both informs and gives the impression of considered analysis. It follows a natural progression then provides a solution. Elegant!

4. **Tell a Story.** Your best "hook," if that is what you're looking for. Stories not only get listeners on board fast. They also release your own expressiveness and ability to persuade in ways that avoid self-consciousness. Because you're emotionally involved, your audience will be too. You'll touch the minds and hearts of your listeners, and your message will come *alive!*

38 Presentation Strategy: Choose a Direct or Indirect Approach

When it comes to delivering your critical message, you have a fundamental choice to make. You can either use a *direct approach* in which you speed straight down the persuasion highway, or an *indirect approach,* which disarms your audience before you drive your message home.

The **direct approach** is simple and efficient. Here, you state your idea, then support or amplify it with evidence and examples. It's straightforward and uncomplicated. Where the correct conditions apply (we'll get to that in a moment), it's definitely the best method to use.

The **indirect approach,** on the other hand, takes a bit more thought and some careful planning. This method is more like a magic act, a sleight of hand, since it involves *building* your argument right in front of your audience's eyes and ears. Though it persuades by a more winding path, it's absolutely the wiser choice in certain situations.

Now let's look at the conditions that apply to each:

Use a **direct approach** when all or most of the following conditions apply:

◆ Your credibility with this audience is high.
◆ Your listeners are positively biased toward you.
◆ Your message is not a sensitive one.
◆ The action you require from the audience is easy for them.

Example: You're the V.P. of Training for a direct selling organization specializing in women's jewelry. Next month's presentation will be a speech to new hostesses on how to organize house parties. You'll be telling them how to succeed in the exciting and profitable world of direct jewelry sales.

An **indirect approach** is a good idea when the above conditions are basically reversed. In such a situation, most or all of these conditions apply:

◆ Your credibility with this audience is low.
◆ Your listeners are negatively biased toward you.
◆ Your message is a sensitive one.
◆ The action required of your audience is difficult.

In these situations, you must establish common ground with your audience then start to build your argument. That strategy allows you to overcome resistance and gain a fair-minded response to your case.

Example: Your group advocates an override in the property tax limitation in an upcoming town election. The money is needed to renovate the town's aging elementary schools. You'll be speaking next week to a group of elderly citizens. You know that these folks are on fixed incomes and no longer have children attending the town's schools. But the override question is sure to be a squeaker, and you need these people to vote "Yes."

You can see how a careful approach, rather than blurting out your controversial message, would help you succeed with this audience. You might, instead, start out by talking about how everyone wants the best for the town and its citizens—including its children—and how you know that this issue is a sensitive one. After establishing common ground in this way, you can start building your case about why your plan is best for everyone, these listeners included.

39 ◆ Staying Cool, Focused, and On Message

It's not about me when I give a presentation... and my friend, it's not about *you* either.

Self-consciousness and sheer nerves make us forget that fact again and again, however. Our focus turns inward, and we forget the critical equation for every talk:

Message + Audience Reception of That Message = Success

What a tremendous relief it is, in fact, when we remove the burden of "being perfect" off our own shoulders! I often use the image of a spotlight to get this point across to clients: When we worry too much about our own performance, we place *ourselves* in a harsh, bright spotlight that can't help but be hot and uncomfortable. Who wouldn't have trouble staying cool in those circumstances?

So why not swivel that spotlight until it's pointing in the right direction, i.e., at your audience! After all, we're supposed to "illuminate" our listeners, aren't we? Practicing this mental trick is another way of reminding ourselves that it's our audience who is supposed to be front and center in a speech.

Another way to stay focused and on message is to allow your energy to flow *out*ward rather than *in*ward. Again, we are turning the tables so that we are more concerned with what is happening with our listeners than with ourselves.

Finally, to ensure that your message has maximum impact, remind yourself that people can only absorb so much information in a short period of time. Keep your data points to a "critical minimum." If you choose *one* vital message, and then come up with at least three forms of evidence that will cement that idea in people's minds, you'll pave the avenue to success.

You may have noticed that that's the very model I've used in this Quick Tip:

My message is the one I started this essay with: "It's not about me and it's not about you." The three points I used to get this idea across were (1) turning the spotlight around to your listeners, (2) allowing your energy to flow outward rather than inward, and (3) choosing one overall message with three forms of evidence to ensure its successful reception.

40 "Simplifying and Selling" Complex Concepts

Need a way to make a complex concept more graspable by your audience? If so, why not borrow a page from the media side of public appearance training?

Why not use a sound bite?

There isn't a reason in the world why sound bites can't be used in speeches and presentations as well as T.V. and radio appearances. They work with in-person listeners the same way they do with media audiences. Their effectiveness as a tool of public speaking depends upon four characteristics:

1. Sound bites use metaphorical language.
2. Sound bites make unexpected comparisons.
3. Sound bites provoke emotional responses.
4. *Sound bites boil a complex concept down to a single vivid image.*

That last point is the important one for this Quick Tip. Here's an example:

Democratic strategist Joe Trippi once said that when a politician picks up a phone with a reporter on the other end, he or she is putting a .357 magnum to their head.

Now *that's* an effective sound bite.

The analogy is crystal clear, and the comparison is an unexpected and therefore an interesting one. It certainly produces an emotional reaction in the listener (in this case, fear). Likewise, "putting a .357 magnum to your head" is a single, vivid image.

All four characteristics are present and are used well. Equally important, the comparison has "simplified and sold" a complex concept.

Republicans know how to use sound bites too. Here's Sen. Everett Dirksen (1896-1969), on Democratic President Lyndon Johnson's military policy in Vietnam: "All the piety of the administration will not put life into the bodies of the young men coming home in wooden boxes."

Here, the unexpected image of piety somehow re-vivifying dead young men is metaphorical language that packs a donkey's kick of emotional power.

There's one more quality a sound bite must have, however. It must achieve some form of elegance—though it may not include propriety or even good taste. In other words, it's possible to include all four of the above components and still come up with a strained image that falls flat because it's just plain clumsy.

Current Senator Dick Durbin's (D-IL) response to the Medicare bill passed just before Thanksgiving in 2003 is an example of a sound bite with rubbery gums and no teeth. The senator opined: "The Republicans will give thanks for this bill, while the American people get stuffed."

Here, the comparison is strained, the use of language infelicitous and clunky. This sound bite wouldn't raise a nibble of anyone's attention.

When you have a complex idea to get across to an audience in a limited amount of time, then, remember the Sound Bite Rule:

Use a comparison that makes your idea come vividly alive, in terms your listeners can understand and relate to.

"Arresting low-level drug users is like bailing out the Atlantic Ocean one teaspoonful at a time." That fits the bill, doesn't it?

You may not achieve sound bite stardom. But you *can* come up with something that helps your audience understand a complex issue a little more easily.

41   Is Your Approach "Stupid" Enough?

Speech—the way *homo sapiens* understand the term—is the uniquely human communication tool. As far as we know, no other species has an instrument of expression that comes close for flexibility, subtly, and levels of complexity.

Animals communicate well enough in the sense of conveying chunks of raw information. An elaborately dancing bee directs other bees to a nectar-laden field of flowers. Whale-calls travel across many miles of ocean in eerie and beautiful soundings. Bird songs differ not only by species, but by "neighborhood," according to the precise geographic location of an individual.

But these forms of communication are not the human vocalizations of speeches, talks, and presentations. We public speakers communicate in much more powerful and subtle ways. We do so not only to classify, differentiate, and warn, as animals do, but to persuade and influence listeners about highly specific issues.

We make a common and significant error in our calculations, however: we tend to think almost exclusively in terms of content: "What is the information I want to get across to my audience?" we constantly ask. In a sense, content is merely raw information of the type that animals use. We need to go further, by effectively using logic and language (i.e., linguistics), two of the tools we alone possess as persuaders.

As I mentioned earlier in this book, our opinion has little

worth unless we back it up with evidence. Similarly, an audience has a hard time being persuaded if it can't follow the logic of the argument offered. As a presenter, you must avoid attempts at persuasion that rest upon fallacies or errors in logic. And since many listeners won't share your commitment to your topic, your argument likewise can't rest upon a leap of faith.

A premise that leads *irrefutably* to a conclusion, on the other hand, is a strong validation of the idea you're presenting. Like a lawyer in court, you must construct an airtight case leading to your ultimate goal of persuasion.

Along with logic, the linguistic side of your speech must be up to par. One way to get it there is to understand that *spoken* language is fundamentally different from the written word. To be effective, your presentation must live and breathe comfortably within its domain.

Spoken sentences should be shorter and simpler than written ones. Words should be concrete rather than abstract. Most often, you'll be better served by sturdy Anglo-Saxon words over their Latinate cousins ("chew" instead of "masticate," "think" rather than "cogitate").

Consider in general whether your language sounds muscular or flabby. Do you use vivid, action-oriented words? Have you built in examples and comparisons to make your points vivid and easy to grasp? Do you tell stories to make your points come alive? Finally, do you include emotional language that resonates on the right side of the brain, where both emotion and decision-making reside?

Deliver a logical argument using powerful language, and your persuasiveness will soar. Remember the mantra that the late Sonny Bono asked himself before a speech: "Is it stupid enough?" He wasn't commenting on the ignorance of his listeners. He was reminding himself to simplify his approach to be as persuasive and influential as possible.

42   Using Rhythm and the Power of Silence

As Quick Tip #41 pointed out, solid logic and muscular language will help give your speeches immediacy and power. To further increase your presentation effectiveness, become aware of the *rhythms* inherent in spoken language, and the advantages of silence.

Let's take silence first. Silence is one of the most powerful tools a speaker can employ, and also the least used. There's no particular reason why business speakers should be aware of the power of silence, but actors certainly understand its effectiveness. At the right moment, silence is a virtual thunderclap.

Most of us are afraid to use silence when we speak, however, because we lack confidence. We think that if a moment (even a few seconds) of silence ensues, our entire speech has gone to hell. The truth is usually just the opposite. The reason we get bored at amateur theatrical productions, for instance, is not that the performers take too much time to deliver their lines, but because they take too little. They don't yet know how to pace the revelation of important information, and they don't understand the depth of everything that's going on in the scene in addition to what the dialogue is expressing.

Experienced speakers know how to use silence as a tool—allowing important points to sink in, or giving audience members a brief space to think on their own. Most important, they understand that a speaker doesn't have to be spinning a ball on every fingertip to keep an audience interested. If we are honest with our listeners and give them a message they need to hear, shouldn't we allow enough time for that message to resonate?

Along with requiring mental breathing space, audiences are keenly attuned to the rhythms of a speaker. Does the person capture the natural *rhythms* of conversational speech? Or is his or her speaking style a mad dash to the end of the performance—

as if they as well as their listeners can't wait to get the whole painful experience over with?

Remember also that the human ear, just like vision, reacts more strongly to change than to sameness. That means that your audience's ears will perk up in the silence that you let settle, and people will understand subconsciously that you've just said something important.

As an added bonus, your listeners will hear confidence when you pause in your delivery. They will recognize that you're a speaker who isn't afraid to let silence speak from time to time. When adrenaline and nervousness kidnap our presentation style, we usually begin to speak like the verbal equivalent of an express train. But audiences don't want to be run down. They'd rather take their time on their journey, and enjoy the view.

43 The Best Kept Secret of PowerPoint

"The Cognitive Style of PowerPoint" is a 2003 monograph by Edward R. Tufte, an expert in the visual display of information. It's a scathing indictment.

Tufte's criticisms of this ubiquitous presentation tool have mostly to do with the "low resolution" of PowerPoint, i.e., the small amount of information that can be included on an individual slide. According to Tufte, "PowerPoint allows speakers to pretend that they are giving a real talk, and audiences to pretend that they are listening."[4]

My own criticisms of PowerPoint concern the fact that it's a presentation device that's virtually guaranteed to *lessen* your influence as a speaker. Since you as presenter are (in

---

[4] Edward R. Tufte, *The Cognitive Style of Power Point* (Cheshire, CT: Graphics Press L.L.C., 2003), 23.

Shakespeare's language) "the be-all and the end-all" concerning the delivery of your critical message, anything that actually reduces your influence is a truly catastrophic state of affairs.

Used as a simple tool of visual information, PowerPoint can be effective. Indeed, in some types of presentations—such as where complex diagrams or moving parts need to be displayed—it may be essential, since such effects can be difficult to achieve otherwise.

Huge problems arise, however, when presenters try to make PowerPoint pack more persuasive firepower than it can deliver. PowerPoint is as effective—and limited—in its narrow range of abilities as a pencil. I happen to love working with lead pencils. But a pencil in a speaker's hand has never convinced me of anything.

Far too often, however, speakers depend upon PowerPoint to achieve some lasting impression on an audience—as if the razzle-dazzle of a multimedia slide show can take the place of an intelligent and compelling argument. Such visual and auditory fireworks, of course, can never replace a dynamic speaker who commands our attention and belief.

Yet there is hope for those who enjoy using Bill Gates's ubiquitous presentation software.

It concerns what I call the *best kept secret of PowerPoint*.

The secret weapon in the war to make PowerPoint a dynamic presentation tool lies in the humble "B" button on our keyboard. Here's how it works:

When you are in the "View" mode of PowerPoint, i.e., when your slides are being projected onto a screen, pressing the "B" button on the keyboard takes your image to *black*. Any screen or surface on which your slides appear—pull-down screen, laptop, or both—will suddenly go completely dark.

When this happens, I guarantee that every one of your audience members will look in the same place: at YOU.

With your audience now paying attention to you instead of

your PowerPoint slides—and you focused entirely on them—real *engagement* can take place. Once again, an organic connection exists between you and your listeners. And so the give-and-take that is essential to the exercise of influence can take place.

I recommend that you go no more than 20 minutes in any presentation before hitting the "B" button and re-engaging your listeners. Ask a question that requires a response. Introduce a group activity. Invite a volunteer to help you with a demonstration.

Try any of these things, or others that you come up with yourself. But hit that "B" button and re-engage with your audience. I think you'll enjoy the people that you'll meet.

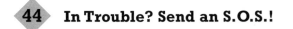

44 In Trouble? Send an S.O.S.!

There will be times when, despite your best positive visualizations beforehand, you'll know that your presentation is sinking fast. That's exactly what happened to me recently, as I conducted a listening skills workshop for 50 judges of the Commonwealth of Massachusetts.

No pressure *there!*

In fact, it was the second time I had conducted this workshop on behalf of a well-known judicial institute. The first time had been to twenty-five judges from a small division of the state's Trial Court. This time, there were not only twice as many jurists, but virtually every department was represented, from the Land Court to the Superior Court.

The difference in the dynamics of the two workshops was dramatic. Unfortunately, I had assumed that the audience and the circumstances of the seminars would be exactly the same, and I was dead wrong.

The first workshop was held on the grounds of an exclusive

prep school with a beautiful suburban campus. My seminar was scheduled for 9 a.m. on the first day of a two-day professional retreat. The participants were expectant and eager to begin their series of workshops.

Now imagine that the scene changes to the second workshop. This time the setting is a law school in a suburb 30-40 minutes from Boston by car (yes, that's *Boston* traffic). The time is 6:00 p.m. on a Wednesday evening. And believe me when I say that a few of those judges looked tired.

But there we were, in a setting not unfamiliar to me. I worked for six years at two Boston law firms, so I'm comfortable in the legal environment.

But not that evening. For one thing, I'm neither a judge nor a lawyer. More important, the jurists in that amphitheater had and have very particular challenges when it comes to listening effectively. And this time, the circumstances of the workshop didn't make them predisposed to listen to me with such a forgiving mind.

Most difficult for me: these judges were clearly hoping to take away *practical* solutions for their very real on-the-job problems. In their thoughts, this was the workshop's priority. And I hadn't realized it. I was primed for a general approach to listening skills in a professional setting; but of course, I had no experience on the bench at all.

Clearly, both the sponsoring organization and I hadn't done our research.

It was a sticky wicket, as the English say. So I did what I advise you to do if you find yourself in a similar situation where your knowledge doesn't match your audience's: open up the issues to the audience members themselves.

Time and again over the next two hours, I offered up a question or a situation I had just been presented with *to the group itself.* I asked my own questions, like these: "Who has experienced a similar situation and how did you resolve it?" "What do you think of what Judge A here did—is that a helpful way to respond to a lawyer who acts like that?" "I'm not sure there is a way to eliminate that problem completely. Can anyone give us a constructive way to handle it?"

In other words, I allowed my experienced and knowledgeable audience members to contribute the information I did not possess. Taking such an approach is not copping out. As a speaker, you are expected to be an expert on your topic, not an omniscient and omnipotent being.

Your audience, in other words, cannot reasonably expect that you will have the answer to every question they ask. Yet sometimes, those unanswered questions seem to pile up in an alarming way.

In these situations, allow your audience to get you out of the jam. Here's a general rule that you can use when you recognize that you're in this situation: *The more specific the questions you are asked, the more likely it is that the audience itself has the answers.* Why shouldn't you use this collective wisdom?

When my workshop was over, many of the participants came up to tell me how gratified they were to even be offered a workshop on listening skills for judges. But I knew how and why I had failed them.

The truth is, at times I turned into more of a facilitator than a trainer. I just figured it was better to do that than to go down with the ship.

◆ ◆ ◆

C H A P T E R

Engaging and Motivating Audiences

◆ ◆ ◆

"I don't care how much a man talks,
if he only says it in a few words."
— JOSH BILLINGS

45 **Four Ways to Captivate Any Audience**

1. **Make eye contact.** Simply put, no behavior is as fundamental
   to persuasion as looking at the person you're talking to. When
   was the last time you trusted somebody who wouldn't look
   you in the eye?

   So actively look at and relate to your audience when you
   speak. (When I say "actively," I mean let your gaze linger for a
   half-a-second to a second. Don't "flick" your eyes at your listeners.) They'll like you more; they'll decide that you're basically honest; and most important, they'll be more willing to be
   influenced by you.

Avoid their gaze just because you're nervous—or weakest excuses, you're busy reading your notes—and you'll have virtually no chance of changing their thinking or behavior.

2. **Enjoy yourself when you speak.** Now *there's* a novel concept! Western culture has imbued public speaking with an aura of inconvenience, horror, and even torture—as if the entire experience belongs in an Edgar Allan Poe story.

   But think about your own experiences as an audience member. Are *you* comfortable listening to a presenter who is clearly embarrassed or fearful?

   A speaker who presents with verve, on the other hand, broadcasts a completely different message. This is a person, we instinctively feel, who has something valuable to say. It *must* be good stuff—look at how much he or she is enjoying talking about it! Pretty soon, we're enjoying ourselves as well.

3. **Smile.** As public speakers, we just plumb don't smile enough. Smiling is another prerequisite to establishing trust with audiences (though it's not as critical as eye contact). At the very least, it's visual evidence of the speaker's enjoyment that I just talked about above.

   In speaking situations where you feel a smile is inappropriate, take one of two alternate paths: (a) "open" your countenance by assuming a pleasant expression; or (b) raise your cheekbones.

   As an illustration of what I mean by this, look at the famous painting *American Gothic*—that's the one of the farmer with his pitchfork, standing next to his wife. Now compare it to the *Mona Lisa*. There's a lady with some raised cheekbones (and look how successful she's been)!

4. **Energize your voice.** Have you ever had to strain to hear what a speaker is saying? Soft-talkers and under-energized presenters make us do more work than we should have to just to hear them. Worse, the speaker seems distant, and we feel left out of the loop.

When you speak, generate enough vocal power and energy to reach every listener in the room—especially people in the back and those who are hard of hearing. (And always assume there will be some of them in your audience.) Remember also that your vocal energy must change in different spaces: the larger the speaking venue, the more you must project your voice. In auditoriums and lecture halls that echo, you'll also have to speak slowly enough for the echo to reach your listeners before you go on.

When you project sufficient energy in a presentation, you make everything easier for your listeners. Now they feel that they can relax, instead of working overtime to do part of your job for you.

46 How to "Read" an Audience and Think on Your Feet

One of the skills of a consummate presenter is the ability to think on one's feet. After all—anyone can give a competent presentation, provided they know their material and have practiced enough.

But what happens when challenging questions and objections start coming your way? Or suppose you're asked to reason your way through a thorny hypothetical situation when you thought you had all the bases covered?

Rather than fear such situations, you should welcome them—for these are precisely the occasions that will prove your mettle as a speaker. If you can grapple with tough questions while retaining a mastery of your subject matter, your credibility and influence with your audience will soar.

It's no wonder, then, that one of the principal tasks of a speech coach is to help presenters think on their feet.

So how is it accomplished?

It's done by bringing not only a fierce level of concentration to your task, but a high level of awareness of what's happening around you. Don't be like the oblivious speaker who buries his nose in his manuscript, or the pompous attorney who reads her entire opening statement from a yellow legal pad.

Instead, *be completely present and paying attention.* A powerful presenter is exactly like the major league baseball player who finds himself up against the league's best pitcher. Both must bear down with 110% attention to what's coming their way.

Here are two ways you can do so:

1. **Listen with your whole being.** Open yourself up completely to the nonverbal communication your audience is giving you. That means using all five (or six) of your senses. For some of us, this involves getting over ourselves so that we can be fully present for our listeners.

   Watch how people are reacting to what you're giving them. Pay attention not only to what they say, but *how they sound* when they say it. Mark their physical response. Especially, have your antennae out to receive their emotional reaction. By reacting in these ways, you'll be fully present to a degree you never imagined possible. Your listeners will not only be impressed—they'll be amazed, because few public speakers are this attentive to their audience.

2. **Expect a reaction.** Most of the time, audience members won't respond actively to what you're saying. Audiences are preconditioned to be passive and unresponsive; and even people who are intensely interested in your topic won't show it outwardly. But you should speak as if you could get a reaction from anyone in the audience *any moment now.*

   Being that focused and ready will keep you fresh and looking responsive in real time. When you do get an externalized reaction, you'll be able to react to it instantly. Just as important, you'll be demonstrating an honest presentation style that shows you're right there with your listeners, every second of the way.

47 Ask Many Small Questions... Okay?

Have you heard that a rhetorical question is a great way to get your audience's attention? Well, it is. The reason is simple: listeners *respond mentally* to questions, whether they think a vocalized answer is expected or not.

Don't you agree?

Questions are speech tools that are custom-made for bridging the gap between audience passivity and a speaker's need to actively engage his or her listeners. The problem is that audiences are conditioned to be passive recipients of information—to sit quietly while information washes over them. As the Eagles song "Hotel California" says: they are programmed to receive.

But people learn poorly in the passive mode. They retain much more when they are active participants in the learning process. An endless procession of PowerPoint slides, for instance, is far more coma-inducing than enlightening.

Questions bring listeners back from this netherworld. Remember the times when you were daydreaming in class and you suddenly heard *your name* called to answer a question? That focused your mind in an instant, didn't it?

Rhetorical or not, questions invite your audience to reacquaint themselves with you, your topic, and your presentation. But there's no need to wait for make-or-break responses to your major points. Even in a 30-minute presentation, there will be dozens of times when you can "ask small questions" to re-engage your audience. Here are some common examples:

"Isn't that so?'"

"Haven't you found that to be the case?"

"You know what I'm talking about, don't you?"

"Yes?"

"Yes or no?"

"We've all experienced that haven't we?"

"Right?"

"Everybody with me so far?"

Any questions?

48   Why Audiences Prefer to See You Naked

Are you an acknowledged expert—perhaps even an authority in your field?

That's nice. But it's not enough where speech performance is concerned.

Many are the movers and shakers, experts all, who failed to connect emotionally with their listeners—to the serious detriment of their speech or presentation.

People like this don't usually lose their jobs because of a bad speech. But they often fail to reach their full potential as communicators. For super-achievers like these, realizing that they lack the ability to be considered warm and likeable can be a monstrous proposition.

Lack of "people skills" is such a huge problem among senior-level executives, in fact, that it keeps one type of executive coach in business.

Getting along with one's audiences and colleagues might seem like a no-brainer, right? The truth is it's actually what we might call a "*half*-brainer."

It's a distinctly left-brain/right-brain problem, you see.

Left-brain analysis and logic can take you far, especially in highly empirical fields like mathematics or the sciences. But when it comes to being influenced in speeches and presentations, it's the right brain that's working overtime in your listeners' minds. Successful talks not only persuade people, but *change their minds in some fashion*—a process that's almost entirely driven by right-brain emotional responses.

You can't be a dynamic communicator, in other words, unless you know how to touch people emotionally.

But there's no need to run out for a quick Ph.D. in Psychology. Simply remember that the ability to influence audiences begins with honesty—and that everything else flows from that starting point. More than anything, that means being fully present in speaking situations, and dealing with your listeners on a human-to-human basis.

You must not only pay attention to how your listeners are receiving your information (so that you can shift gears if necessary). You must also take chances, remaining open and vulnerable rather than going for cheap effects. Nakedness may be frightening to a performer, but it's always more interesting for an audience than a cover-up.

49 How to Move an Audience to Action

Getting your audience to actually *do* something—or to change their thinking—is a key ingredient to achieving influence as a speaker. Yet it is all too easy to become overly focused on the content of our presentations and to miss the actionable part completely. "What can I say," we ask ourselves with near desperation, "that will keep people interested?"

But "interested" is a state of mind and nothing more. We must ask ourselves instead how we want to affect our listeners— to leave them better off as a result of our presentation. Such thinking requires a different type of planning on our part.

We are taking a huge step up by doing so—from merely

delivering important information, to getting our audiences to behave differently as a result of what we say to them. The mechanism to accomplish this significant result is simple: Ask yourself what you want your listeners to think, feel, or do as a result of your speech. Now you're walking a path that will yield actual results.

Let's see an example of how this works:

You're scheduled to give a speech on helping to reverse global warming. Interesting? Yes. An important topic? Of course. But your speech can engage and motivate your listeners in many different ways, depending on the action you require at the end of it.

Do you want them to analyze a specific aspect of the problem and conduct research?

Write a letter to the editor of their local paper?

Sign a petition to the governor?

Buy a more fuel-efficient car?

Begin recycling?

Start an Earth Day awareness campaign in their town?

Ride public transportation one day a week?

Make a financial contribution to your organization?

Start a legal advocacy group?

Stop using spray deodorant?

Every one of these choices, once you aim for it as an actionable result of your speech, requires a significant shift in your own thinking. The action you require of your listeners will dictate the approach, tone, organization, forms of evidence used, emotional climate, degree of fervor, and many other factors in your presentation.

When you understand exactly how you want your audience to react, you'll begin to think in terms of using any and all tools to make that happen. You'll be thinking and speaking strategically.

50 Curtain Up! Add Drama to Your Speech

When was the last time you sat through a truly memorable presentation? I'm talking about a speech with fresh ideas and true feelings, movingly delivered, and a clear (and exciting) sense that the topic really mattered.

Perhaps you've *never* experienced a presentation like that. If you have, the odds are excellent that you remember it.

As you conceive your presentations, ask yourself where the *drama* exists in your talk. Drama moves audiences like nothing else in the world. Speeches with drama deal with human beings facing challenges and conflicts—and finding ways to overcome them.

Look back on your own life and determine where the drama lies. It's easiest to understand the power that a dramatic story can pack through the events of our own life.

Now transfer that sense of highs and lows to your product, service, mission, or whatever else your topic may be. Who was facing defeat, but won? Who took the bravest chance and in the end prevailed? Think power, conflict, heroes, quests, adventures, underdogs, dark deeds, white steeds, and against-all-odds triumphs—*these* are some of the ingredients of drama.

And don't imagine these things exist only in fairy tales and action films. The story you want to tell is filled with them. They're the stuff of struggles and successes on behalf of people in need—including customers, clients, and constituents. You know all about that, don't you?

So start digging for that gold.

51 Dynamic Presenters Tell Stories. Do You?

I'll never forget how I learned one of life's great lessons: Seize every opportunity that comes your way to get an education. Or to say it another way: Don't be stupid enough to let educational opportunities go by so that you *stay* stupid.

Here's how my learning experience took place:

I was in high school. Well, not that day I wasn't. My friend Ron and I had decided to accompany a guy named Wild Willie from our hometown of New Bedford, Mass. to Connecticut.

Wild Willie (no tip-off in that name, nossir!) was a high-school dropout who was crazy about cars and street-fights and spent every cent he had on wrecks that he'd tinker around with and somehow get rolling again.

On that particular day, Wild Willie was headed to Hartford to apply for a factory worker's job at the Pratt & Whitney aircraft engine manufacturing plant. Naturally, this exciting quest soon acquired two eager passengers.

That January day was bitterly cold, and not long after we set out on the three-hour drive it began to snow. We reached Hartford without incident and Wild Willie successfully completed his application (a feat in itself, I'm sure). But the roads on our return journey were now snow-covered and treacherous.

Wild Willie drove as usual, though—crazily—and somewhere along Route 95 we spun out at 60 or 70 miles an hour. At first the car introduced itself to the guardrail on our right side with only a passing handshake; but then we immediately spun around 360 degrees, and the Williemobile grabbed that guardrail with spirit and conviction, from the front this time, as though it was greeting an old friend that had been away for a *long* time.

The Williemobile now resembled an accordion on wheels; though miraculously, no one was hurt. But the car was totaled.

Suddenly, we were without transportation in another state, in a blinding snowstorm, without adequate clothing or protection of any kind.

A Connecticut state trooper gave us a ride to the Massachusetts line and dropped us off at a restaurant plaza there. (I am not making this up.) So there we were: stranded 100 miles from home, forced to use our blue thumbs to hitch a ride northwards.

We managed to get a lift to the outskirts of Boston, where I phoned my dad with the entirely reasonable request that he drive 50 miles in a heavy snow squall to pick us up.

You can imagine his first question on getting such a call from his son on a school day.

Wild Willie didn't get the job, by the way. But for once, I heard wisdom in what my dad was saying to the three of us on the hour-long ride home through the snows of hell. I recall that it had something to do with staying in school and the value of an education.

Too bad it was such a hard lesson. But life's like that sometimes, isn't it?

As I say, dear reader, that's a true story. Would it work as part of a speech to high-school students on the importance of staying in school? Probably.

The reason? *Nothing grabs an audience and keeps them engaged like a good story.* We see our own lives as the story of our existence—a chronological tale of one person's time on Earth. As such, we measure the phenomenon of time in a forward direction, as that story and others that we experience appear to unfold in our minds.

Stories give all of us—speaker and audience members alike—a sense of control in a world where we desperately need control.

But stories play another crucial role for us as presenters: they show us at our very best. When we're actively involved in telling an interesting tale, we shine in terms of liveliness, commitment to our message, passion, involvement, and the sheer force of our personality.

So tell the story of your company, organization, product, or idea. Discuss the real needs of the people involved in this story, and how they were met or still need to be met. Speak of challenges faced and obstacles overcome; the hopes and steadfast commitment to a dream that succeeded at last; the continuing desires of the people whose story you've just told; or anything else that puts human beings at the center of your message.

Dynamic presenters tell stories about the things that really matter. You should, too.

52 Speaking Visually in the Age of Television

Do you know what the greatest persuader in the world is?

It isn't a person.

It's *television*.

Over the past half-century, television has fundamentally transformed public discourse and altered the way we respond to critical information. It has accomplished this by teaching us that important information always comes with some kind of visual reinforcement.

The implication of this for speeches and presentations is clear: *Presentation excellence in the 21st century requires a strong visual component.*

In fact, it isn't only television that's changing our perceptions. Video games, BlackBerries, cell phone-cameras, and shape-shifting billboards are doing their part daily, even hourly. Audience members, in other words, are already awash in a sea of visual information. And since they seem to be swimming along splendidly, we'd better learn how to put our speech-oars in the water.

Fortunately, as presenters we already have considerable visual resources at our disposal. Most important among these, perhaps, is *our self.* We are really our most effective visual aid.

Another highly effective visual component to speeches and presentations is stories.

I mentioned in Quick Tip #51 that stories show us at our most personable and communicative. They also present the perfect opportunity to speak in visual terms, since they unfold as a series of pictures in our listeners' minds. Novelists learned some time ago how to mimic the cinematic-inspired visual unfolding of a story. We presenters need to learn how to do likewise.

PowerPoint and other visual presentation tools offer us one way to do so. But an equally effective tactic is to create "word-pictures" in the minds of your audience. For instance, note the difference in the following two openings of a speech on globalization:

Opening A:

"Good morning. I'm delighted to be here with the representatives of the Pan-American Trade Council. This conference reinforces for me the progress your country has made recently in its efforts at globalization. The statistics clearly show how many more indigenous goods we're seeing from this nation in the global marketplace."

Opening B:

"Good morning. I'm delighted to be here with the representatives of the Pan-American Trade Council. You know, on the way over here, we drove by one of your local farmers markets. And I must say I was amazed at the variety of goods I saw there.

We saw handmade clothing in vibrant tropical patterns, rows of brightly-painted ceramics, and the luscious colors of the tropical fruits. For me it was a powerful reminder that your country has truly entered the global marketplace."

When we speak visually like this, we conjure up vivid representations in the minds of audience members. Not only that—but such imagery allows listeners to construct their own *personal* visuals out of the experiences of their lives. The "brightly painted ceramics" that you see in the speech example above are different from the ones that I see, and likewise with every member of the audience.

Almost no other technique allows you to reach that level of personalization with your listeners. And don't forget that decisions (including being persuaded) take place in the "right brain"—the same hemisphere where visual imagery resides.

Now, picture how important *that* knowledge is for you as a speaker.

CHAPTER

Dealing with Skeptical Audiences and Resistance

◆ ◆ ◆

53 **Know Your Listeners' Needs and Expectations**

"The secret of being a bore is to tell everything."
— *Voltaire*

Understanding who your listeners are and what they expect from you is essential to persuading them. This knowledge is particularly useful for audiences who are skeptical or resistant to your message.

If that is the case, ask yourself the following four sets of questions beforehand. The answers will benefit you with any audience, but they will be especially helpful with skeptical or resistant groups of listeners:

◆ Who are you trying to influence in this presentation?

- Is it the people actually in the room or auditorium?
- Is it, instead, bosses, board members, or other opinion leaders not present?
- Are there other behind-the-scenes decision-makers to be concerned about?
- Should your primary influence be aimed at representatives of the media?
- Is speaking to the community at large the smarter move at this point?
- Are there political considerations that supersede your actual presentation?

The central question here, then, is this: Are the people in the room the ones you really need to convince—or is it someone else?

◆ What do these people know and expect in this speaking situation?
- What is the audience's knowledge of your topic?
- How much essential information should you be trying to get across? (Avoid an "information dump!")
- Do your listeners have clear expectations concerning your presentation?
- What are their preferences concerning presentation style and the level of engagement and participation?

Here, you need discipline! You must speak at the appropriate level of knowledge, including only critical information. Do your homework. Can you obtain information about previous presentations to this group? What did those speakers do, and were their efforts successful? Why or why not?

◆ What is the emotional context of the occasion?
- Is there any bias toward or against you, your topic, or your organization?

- Are the attendees here voluntarily or not?
- Is there an emotional context (recent disasters, a crisis, lay-offs, etc.) you should know about?
- Do cultural issues apply?
- Are your organization's *values* important to this audience?
- How easy or difficult is the action you're asking of them as a result of your presentation?

Emotions and values can be critical factors in your success as a presenter, and you ignore them at your peril. Does this prospective customer or audience have a worldview that is central to their reception of your message? Has anything occurred in their world recently that will positively or negatively impact their receptivity?

◆ How will your message benefit these listeners?
  - What is the relationship of your topic to their professional or personal lives?
  - Do you include practical knowledge or skills they can use immediately?
  - Does your talk foster group cohesion and motivation?
  - Is your good will completely evident to them?

Your listeners must believe that you are speaking for *their* benefit, not your own. Is that message getting through to your audience loud and clear?

54 Understand the Culture You're Dealing With

What does the word "culture" elicit in your mind in terms of audiences? For many of us, a culture refers to a clearly defined geographical or national grouping: the Bedouin, Tibetans, the cowboys of the American West.

Ruth Fulton Benedict, a cultural anthropologist, had this to say about this interpretation of culture:

> *From the moment of his birth the customs into which [an individual] is born shape his experience and behavior. By the time he can talk, he is the little creature of his culture.* (Patterns of Culture. *Mariner Books, reissue edition, 1989.)*

Whole libraries exist on communicating within this definition of culture—books concerning gestures and taboos, global business practices, and protocols required for social and professional interaction. If you conduct business globally, or you're a diplomat, social services volunteer, or you're called upon to give speeches abroad, this is an area in which you would do well to educate yourself.

But many *audience* cultures exist that have nothing to do with geography or political boundaries. These are often sub-cultures within a larger population. The cultural categories can be large—religious, racial, occupational, gender, political—or more finely differentiated: a social network, a club or fraternal order, a collection of hobbyists, or simply a group of interested individuals.

Companies and organizations have their own sub-cultures as well. A speech to the sales department of a large corporation will probably require a different approach than one to regional distribution managers gathering for their once-a-year meeting at the national headquarters.

The expectations of such well-defined groups can differ dramatically where a speaker is concerned. Sometimes that difference will impress itself on you as merely an interesting homogeneity of thought and action. But at other times, a palpable resistance may be evident.

When speaking to cultures that are different from your own,

try to understand as accurately as possible the expectations of your audience. In broad cultural categories, this may mean simply respecting hierarchies and levels of authority. In more finely sliced cultural categories, however, succeeding often comes down to understanding the specific likes and dislikes of the group and the mechanics of the presentation itself.

Does this audience prefer a lecture or interactive exercises? Do they want details, or should you cut to the chase immediately? Do they like an open-ended discussion or does the prospect horrify them?

Will they be respectful or aggressive in responding to your message? How will you deal with either outcome?

Perhaps most importantly, make sure you strongly establish your own credibility. Mention your credentials, experience, or accomplishments. And don't shy away from naming influential individuals you've worked with in this area.

Since you're not a member of this culture, listeners will need persuading concerning why they should listen to you. Give them solid reasons at the start, when they're making their critical judgments about you.

55 Seven Tips for Overcoming Resistance

If you haven't read the previous two entries in this book—Quick Tips #53 and 54—I recommend you do so now. Those pages discuss ways to understand your audience's knowledge, expectations, and cultural biases. They give you resources for overcoming resistance by helping you strategize and prepare beforehand.

Now I'd like to discuss resistance that you can't anticipate—the kind that rears its fearsome head during your presentation.

The first thing worth understanding concerning challenges

from an audience is that you shouldn't fear them. Salespeople understand that quibbles—and even clear disagreements—are often the necessary steps toward a successful sale. It's the same with presentations and the audiences that hear them.

Questions and objections mean, for one thing, that listeners are remaining engaged with you and your topic. They haven't shut themselves off and stopped listening to your argument. That's a critical point in your favor.

Resistance is a natural element of thinking and attentive audiences. Therefore we mustn't resist it too strenuously. We lose a considerable part of our persuasiveness when we adopt a "siege mentality," believing that we're continually dodging flaming arrows hurtling our way over the battlements.

The instant we shift from reaching out toward our listeners, to defensiveness, we lose control of the situation—and it shows. From that point on, we've stopped advocating effectively on behalf of our message.

So stay positive and hopeful! Audiences generally respect a speaker who stands up for his or her beliefs in the face of determined resistance. Here are seven practical ways you can gain that respect and still deliver your message effectively:

1. **Understand the type of resistance you're facing.** Is it institutional or personal? Fact-driven or cultural? An ego trip for the questioner or a flaw in your logic? *Be alert to what's coming your way, but respond honestly.* Your credibility with your listeners will stay strong, and perhaps even improve.

2. **Listen for emotions.** My emotional state as an audience member can be a major reason why I'm resisting your message. You represent a point of view; a company; the way things are usually done, etc. Therefore, you provide a convenient target for me to attempt to redress a recent problem, or to vent after decades of resentment and anger. Even in the absence of such an emotional storm, there may be subtle con-

notations in what I say to you as speaker that you would do well to listen for so that you can respond appropriately.

3. **Recast erroneous assumptions.** The more damaging an erroneous assumption expressed by an audience member, the sooner you must respond. This may even mean interrupting the questioner. It can be done nicely ("Excuse me, but I can't agree... "). But it's vital that you set the record straight as soon as possible. Otherwise the faulty argument sits in the minds of the audience, slowly setting like concrete.

4. **Welcome unclear or fuzzy arguments.** Yes: if the logic of your opponents is faulty, or their arguments are simply so much debris floating in the vastness of space... you win! Accept this gift, and use the objection to take your argument in any direction you choose. You may, for instance, state the strongest argument of your case all over again.

5. **Go low-key and conversational.** The more an audience member rants and tries to provoke an emotional response from you, the quieter you should become. Take your time in answering; be logical and patient and kind. Your demeanor will favorably highlight your reasonableness in contrast to your opponent's apoplexy.

6. **Be aware of your tone.** As I stated above, incorrect assumptions and damaging assertions must be countered as quickly as possible. But the best arguments in the world will fail if you sound defensive or angry as you respond. *Audiences will remember the tone of your presentation far longer than they will recall facts and statistics.* Remember that nearly forty percent of message receptivity resides in the sound of your voice alone!

7. **Disagree neutrally.** Many opportunities will arise with recalcitrant audience members for you to demonstrate your rapier wit. Resist every one of them, for the reasons given above.

56   Be a S.A.N.E. Speaker

As speakers, we like to think we'll have a positive effect even when listeners are resistant. The sobering reality, however, is that very few presenters achieve such influence. Most talks and speeches are just like all the *other* talks on this issue. They show little creativity or boldness. And so they fail where the crucial requirement of influencing listeners is concerned.

So what can we do as speakers to establish rapport and reach such listeners in some actionable way, despite skepticism and resistance?

We can remain S.A.N.E. by remembering to do the following:

Shape the issue: You give yourself a tremendous advantage as a speaker when you frame your message in ways that work to your advantage. In fact, it's difficult to overcome skepticism and resistance *unless* you do so.

Consider the example of a classic management-labor dispute. Union leaders invariably present the issue as either a) a "fair shake" for the working man and woman, or b) a case of Big Business vs. the little guy. (Often, of course, they use both arguments simultaneously.)

Company officials typically will raise the question of fairness as well, by asking a question like this one: "Are the union's demands fair compared to what ordinary Americans are getting in terms of wages and benefits?" Or they will frame the situation in even starker terms, warning that the company won't survive if the union's demands are met. Both sides in a labor-management dispute thus consciously shape the issue to their own advantage.

Areas of agreement: Your influence with a resistant audience depends on whether you can establish common ground with them. And the earlier you do so, the better.

Once audience members understand that you're all working toward a common goal, they'll be much more likely to view you as a person of integrity. This is important, even if—and especially if—your views differ from theirs. You'll be a speaker who's at least worth listening to. Who of us can ask any more?

New approaches: People who resist your point of view will be convinced they've already heard all the arguments on your side. So surprise them. Give them something they haven't heard before.

It needn't be a radical departure from past presentations, though it might be. At any rate, focus on stories and metaphors as you make your case. Above all, use comparisons your audience can understand.

An audience of salespeople I trained recently, for instance, was delighted to hear that *silence* was as important in persuading a prospect as anything they said (since customers need a fraction of a second for each critical point to sink in). I used the comparison of Zen masters who tell us to look at the space between objects instead of the objects themselves. It was an unexpected but apt comparison.

Of course, this means that you need to do your homework to understand who your listeners are and how they think.

Emotions. We hold the beliefs we do because we think they are the right beliefs, the ones that correspond to our values. And that involves a strong emotional component. If you want to change people's convictions or behavior, you won't do it with statistics and pie charts. You have to speak about your issue in ways that touch people's lives.

Don't be afraid to reveal, for instance, how *you* have wrestled with this issue. You'll be giving them permission to do the same, and perhaps come out of the struggle on your side of the question.

57 **Defuse Your Opponents' Arguments**

When we hear the word "argument," we often think of disagreement and contentiousness. Yet the first definition of argumentation in my office dictionary is "the process of arriving at reasons and conclusions."[5]

The process of arriving at reasons and conclusions.

What a different meaning from the commonly understood one! And what an opportunity to use the tools of logic and evidence discussed earlier in this book.

For, if influencing listeners depends upon making the better argument—as it does from elections to advertising—then recognizing your opponents' line of reasoning can be a critical factor in your success.

You might say it's a process of defusing your opponents' "bombs" before they're thrown your way.

Lawyers certainly know this. If a client harbors a skeleton in the closet, and the opposing side knows about it, the attorney will often bring it up first with his or her own client on the stand. The theory is that a weakness you reveal yourself will do less damage than it would if trumpeted by your enemies.

Similarly, when an organization is in the midst of a crisis, the worst thing it can do is to withhold damaging information so that it leaks out drip by corroding drip. Everyone knows that it wasn't the burglary itself but the cover-up that brought down the Nixon administration.

The same advice holds for you as a speaker. By raising your opponents' objections first, you can deflate them with the argument you've prepared beforehand. That's almost impossible to do with, say, a question from the audience that blindsides you.

---

[5] David B. Guralnik, Editor in Chief, *Webster's New World Dictionary* (New York: Simon and Schuster, 1980), 74.

You've often heard experienced speakers using this tactic, saying something like this: "The other side says we shouldn't take this course of action. But let's look at what would happen if we were to take their advice."

So think of the strongest or most likely objections to your position, including from audience members you expect to be resistant. Then come up with your most powerful case to *prove those arguments wrong.*

Employ the principles of evidence, reasoning, emotion, logic, language, and effective delivery that I've talked about throughout this book.

If you're successful, you may hear that most beautiful of sounds: minds changing.

CHAPTER

Handling Q & A Like a Pro

◆ ◆ ◆

58 Q & A: The Forgotten Avenue to Audience Persuasion

What's your relationship with the question-and-answer session that typically follows a speech or presentation? Which of the following two main camps do you reside in?

Camp Concern:
I feel confident in my talk itself. But I dread what follows, since *I can't anticipate the questions that will be coming my way!!*

Or

Camp Coping:
I relish the opportunity at last to engage the people in the room. *Now at last we can have a real dialogue about my topic!!*

Whichever of these two camps feels like home to you—or

even if neither of them do—remember that question-and-answer sessions are golden opportunities for persuasion and influence.

That's because Q & A offers a platform for stating your message all over again while presenting yourself at your professional best. Anyone can give a good speech if they know their topic and they've prepared sufficiently. But few speakers can handle themselves with consummate grace in the rough-and-tumble of audience reactions to their views or their performance.

You need to be one of them.

To understand how challenging Q & A sessions work to your advantage as a speaker, picture the following scenario:

You're an audience member who's just listened to an excellent presentation by an authority on this topic. Now the speaker announces that he or she will take questions.

Usually, one of three things happens at some point (or they *all* happen):

1. An audience member asks a devilishly difficult and insightful question, one that's so good you wish you'd thought of it yourself;
2. Someone stands up and begins pontificating at such length that you're embarrassed for the speaker;
3. The person right behind you starts attacking the speaker in a personal and nasty manner, while you attempt to dematerialize out of sheer embarrassment.

How the speaker responds in each of these scenarios depends upon many factors. These include the topic and speaking situation, the speaker's reputation and personality, the make-up of the audience, the intimacy of the talk, and so on.

One fact, however, remains constant: the person who handles himself with professionalism and aplomb in each of these scenarios *grows in stature and credibility* with the entire audience.

Q & A, in other words, offers a priceless opportunity for you to shine in ways that your presentation—where you basically interact with no one—simply doesn't.

Let's look at some of the specific opportunities afforded by Q & A:

◆ It allows you to strongly reinforce or amplify your message.
◆ It's your last chance to make a positive impression on your audience. (This is especially important if you've encountered difficulties in your presentation itself.)
◆ It allows you to provide essential information that a) wasn't included in your presentation itself, or b) wasn't sufficiently clear to the audience. And remember, if one person doesn't understand something, many more people who couldn't summon the courage to ask the question in public are probably also confused.
◆ It gives you the opportunity to issue your "call to action."

So whether you're a Q & A lover or hater, remember that the question-and-answer session isn't just the tail-end of your presentation. It's a strategic tool, to be used for further persuasion and influence.

59 What if Nobody's Asking Questions?

Ask any actor if they have a recurring nightmare, and the answer will almost certainly be: "I dreamed I was on stage on opening night and I couldn't remember my lines."

Sounds clichéd, perhaps. But it's still enough to make any performer wake up in a cold sweat. I left the theater two decades ago and I still get that one from time to time.

Public speakers have their own nightmare, and it sounds like this: "I finish my speech and start the Q & A... and *nobody asks a single question!"*

As it happens, the speaker's nightmare is worse than the actor's. Actors occasionally *do* forget their lines, of course. But it usually isn't for very long; and any competent actor will be able to recover in character without the audience being any the wiser. (The best performers can improvise in iambic pentameter in the middle of a scene of Shakespeare's!)

The actor's nightmare, then, stays mostly in the world of unpleasant nocturnal fantasies.

Not so the public speaker's dilemma. We've all been in situations when no one volunteers a question after we've finished a speech. In fact, it's a pretty common occurrence.

Here are four remedies, dear reader, for this situation that I know you fear more than the return of the Bubonic Plague:

Solution #1 ("Show and tell"): When you say, "Does anyone have any questions?" raise your own hand. This gives listeners permission to follow your lead; and anyway, it's visual reinforcement (see Quick Tip #23, "Your Best Visual Aid is... *You!*").

Solution #2 ("The Salvage Operation"): Bring up an earlier comment or question. You can say, for instance: "Well, in this morning's segment, this gentleman asked whether... "

The salvaged question may be something you didn't have time to address previously. It might also be a comment you mentally saved in your "Favorites" file for just such an occurrence. So start listening closely to comments made by audience members, either during your speech or on the coffee break. You may be able to use them later in Q & A.

Solution #3 ("Does anyone have any questions for my answers?"): That line is actually Henry Kissinger's at a press conference, and I think it's perfect for this strategy. Seize the moment (since apparently, no one else will) and ask the question yourself!

You might say something like: "Well, I'm often asked. . ." or

"One of the things people wonder about this subject is... " Have at least a half-dozen of these home-baked questions ready to pop out of your presentation toaster when the time is right. Just remember that they should be used at intervals during Q & A, not one after the other.

Solution #4 ("Desperate times require desperate measures"): Throw in an activity that will involve everyone. Basically anything is fair game, as long as it doesn't appear to be *punishment for not asking any questions.*

You could say, for example: "Great! This gives us the opportunity to do something I was hoping we'd be able to get to. Everyone please turn to the person on your left. . ." and away you go.

Whichever of the above solutions you choose should be initiated speedily. Nothing is worse than a long painful pause, punctuated with remarks such as, "C'mon, SOMEBODY has to have a question!" or "Isn't anybody wondering about such-and-such?"

The good thing about these remedies is that they will grease the wheels so that questions start rolling your way. And if not, that's okay, because I have this activity... .

60 ⬥ 4 Reasons to Love Q & A Sessions

If you've read the previous two Quick Tips, you should at least be on speaking terms with question-and-answer sessions. You're aware that Q & A is an excellent avenue of persuasion. And you know some techniques for starting the ball rolling with questions following your presentation.

Now I'd like to convince you of why you should look forward to the Q & A period, because of the benefits it can bring to your speeches.

The greatest of these is that Q & A gives you the chance to

enrich and deepen listeners' experience of your talk. That in itself should be refreshing for both you and your audience. Yet there are at least four more reasons why you should love Q & A. Here they are:

Reason # 1: Your presentation may have confused some audience members or left them unconvinced. Or worse, left them unimpressed with you as a speaker.

In such cases, Q & A is your golden opportunity to either continue to inform and convince—or to do so at last as you conclude your presentation. Remember that speakers who handle themselves with style and assuredness in the rough-and-tumble of Q & A may win over some listeners for the first time!

Reason # 2: It's your chance to clarify your argument, give examples of your solution in action, or overcome opposition.

Most of the time, we're challenged to cram essential information into a too-brief presentation period. Because Q & A gives the appearance of being audience controlled rather than speaker controlled, it allows you to expand your argument while responding directly to your listeners "off the clock." The atmosphere created should feel more relaxed, while giving you greater scope to deepen your audience's understanding.

Reason #3: Q & A is more conversational and natural than a one-way speech.

All effective public speaking is *conversational*, since audiences want speakers to communicate with them honestly, openly, and in everyday language. Too often, speeches have the feeling of a monologue, delivered through a one-way dynamic to a polite but anesthetized crowd of onlookers.

The back-and-forth of Q & A should feel more comfortable to you AND your listeners. Best of all, when you're *conversing* about a topic you truly care about, all of your best qualities as a speaker will emerge.

Reason #4: Q & A demands your absolute best.

Let's face it: A question-and-answer period is a tremendous challenge. We can practice our presentations to our heart's content—but we can never know what queries and objections may come our way when we invite our listeners to respond.

To excel in Q & A, you have to be 100% focused and able to think nimbly on your feet; sensitive to your audience's feelings and opinions; and empathetic concerning individual questioners' points of view. Oh, and you must remain spontaneous, flexible, logical, and good-natured.

Accomplish all of this—with a dash of humor tossed in if you can manage it—and you may surpass the effectiveness of your presentation itself.

 **61 The 7 Danger Zones of Q & A**

Earlier in this chapter, I said that Q & A is one of the most challenging aspects of public speaking. Yet it's also one of your greatest opportunities to shine as a presenter.

If you can field questions with panache, think on your feet, and marshal pieces of evidence with only seconds' notice, you'll convince listeners that you are at the top of your game.

That's not to say that audiences—including journalists, if they happen to be present—will make it easy for you. In fact, Q & A sessions tend to bring out the worst and sometimes the angriest of our critics. So prepare yourself beforehand for a few self-propelled grenades that will probably be heading your way.

What follows in this Quick Tip is your own ammunition toolbox. It's part of the segment of my workshops I call "The 7 Danger Zones of Q & A." It's a brief explanation of the worst types of questions you will face in question-and-answer sessions, with comments about how you can best cope with each one.

"The 7 Danger Zones"

1. Hostile questions
2. Loaded questions
3. Leading questions
4. Hypothetical questions
5. Multifaceted questions
6. Fuzzy questions
7. False choices

1. **Hostile Questions:** Hostile questions often reflect pent-up anger directed at you simply because you're a convenient target. *"I've been dealing with salespeople like you for 30 years, and I'm sick and tired of"*... has very little to do with your personal style, personality, or competence.

   The key to handling hostility from questioners is to stay in control emotionally, and to listen carefully to what is behind or underneath the question. (In the theater, we call this critical information the *subtext* to what is being spoken aloud.) Try to grasp the emotional context or underlying problem, and address yourself to that as much as possible.

   Remember also that responding to hostile questions means continuing your objective of *persuasion*. Your chief purpose is still to advance the goals of your presentation, not to parry your opponents' attacks with a dazzling display of swashbuckling skills.

2. **Loaded Questions:** Loaded questions are exactly what they sound like: explosive. And as the speaker, you are being invited to light the fuse! Since loaded questions are filled with damaging assumptions and conclusions, your job is similar to a Bomb Squad officer's: You must defuse the charge and bring the situation under control.

   Most important, *you must recast the assumption that is harming your case into different language.* "Well, I can't agree with your interpretation that . . ." or "First, I have to correct something that you just said," are two options you can use, or similar phrasing.

An important rule: The more damaging the assumption voiced by the questioner (that the entire audience hears, after all), the quicker you must refute it. If that means interrupting the questioner in the middle of the so-called-question-but-really-an-attack, go right ahead.

3. **Leading Questions:** A leading question is one in which the preferred answer is embedded in the question itself. "Isn't it true that... ?" is a classic opening to a leading question, since the questioner obviously believes that "it" is true.

This is a sweet deal for the questioner, since it involves asking and answering the question simultaneously! But you mustn't let it happen. Again, listen carefully, so that you can hear when the questioner has slipped in his or her own assumptions. That's the time to recast any damaging assumptions or assertions (see point #2, above).

4. **Hypothetical Questions:** These are really "swamp" questions, since they usually lead you into a fog-enshrouded bog that's impossible to find your way out of. So why go there at all?

A simple standard response of, "I can't answer a hypothetical question like that" should suffice. The one exception to this advice is to go ahead and answer if the hypothetical situation makes a point you'd like to be heard.

For instance, when Condoleezza Rice said the United States would consider it "a grave threat" if North Korea tested a nuclear device, the Bush administration obviously wanted to get that message out. As you can imagine, diplomats and negotiators use this option in responding to hypotheticals all the time.

5. **Multifaceted Questions:** This too-many-bites-at-the-apple transgression appears frequently, particularly among journal-

ists. The challenge here is that the many facets of the question(s), or the sheer length of the diatribe which precedes the actual question (if there is one), can make these interrogatories a real challenge. Even that last sentence tested your patience, didn't it?

Multifaceted questions can work to your advantage, however. That's because they allow you to answer as many of the facets as you like while ignoring the rest. If the question is long enough or convoluted, the audience probably won't notice what you've left out!

You can also take advantage of a multifaceted question by going directly to your main talking points, thereby restating your critical message. Again, the questioner has opened the door for you by behaving unreasonably and impractically.

6. **Fuzzy Questions:** This one is an All-Time-Greatest-Hits candidate for T.V. interviews and radio call-in shows. When a questioner's thinking is as sharp as the surface of a tennis ball, you should basically give thanks to your Higher Power, and take your answer in any direction you like. You may also ask for a more targeted question from that person, but why give up the chance to state your message all over again?

7. **False Choices:** A false choice is an example of a fallacy, or an error in reasoning: "Look, we've got to use the state educational funds for either a new gym or an auditorium. Those are the things we need, and we can't afford both. So let's make up our minds!"

Why are those the *only* two choices? In reality, there are probably at least a dozen options in such a situation. When someone offers you a false choice, simply point out that there are, in fact, other alternatives, and then begin to discuss your favorites.

62 How to Tackle a Question-Hog

You know that person who monopolizes your time during Q & A, asking follow-up after follow-up to his original question? How about the pontificator who gives a lengthy treatise *as an introduction* to the question he eventually asks? Or the person who's more interested in broadcasting the depth of her knowledge than actually inquiring about anything?

These people are Question-Hogs.

As a speaker, you have to keep these critters in their pen where they belong.

The way you do it is by exercising control.

Question-hogs aren't just a Q & A nuisance—they have the potential to disrupt the entire time management of your question-and-answer session. They keep you from building momentum or flow. They put fellow audience members into an irreversible coma. And they vote the wrong way in every single election!

We can agree, then, that you have to stop Question-Hogs in their tracks. You therefore have permission to use your ultimate weapon:

Eye contact.

Here's how it works: When a Question-Hog asks a question, you *begin* your response while looking directly at the questioner. Very soon, however, you "open up" your answer to the entire barnya-- er, audience. Now you're looking at everyone except the questioner. Most important, that's where you conclude your answer.

You thus have plausible deniability concerning the person who's waving her arm frantically in the air (i.e., the Question-Hog). You're looking at the other side of the auditorium by now, so YOU DON'T EVEN SEE HER.

Of course, you do notice the hand of the polite questioner on that side of the room who's been patiently waiting for her turn.

Despite what your spouse says, you see, a roving eye is a good thing.

Just don't tell said spouse that I told you that.

◆63◆   Emerging from Q & A As a Winner

Here's a way to conclude your Q & A sessions dynamically and convincingly. It generally will boost your credibility with your audiences, and best of all, it's simple to remember.

In fact, it's as easy as "1-2-3."

That's because you never say: "I have time for *one* [or *two* or *three*] more question(s)."

You're not that dangerously specific. Here's why:

What if the last question (if you said, "We have time for one more") is a nightmare, involving a dilemma Solomon himself couldn't untangle? Is that the way you want to end your make-or-break presentation?

Or suppose you're giving a sales talk, and Questioner #2 (since you invited "Two more") seizes upon the opportunity to accuse your company of turning out overpriced junk for the past twenty years?

Or what if the final contribution from the audience (the third of "Three more"... hey, you asked for it!) reveals the one weakness in your argument that you were really, really hoping you wouldn't be asked about?

You see the point, don't you?

Now for the simple solution:

Instead of trapping yourself with, "We have time for one last question," say something like: "We have time for *a few more* questions."

Then end the Q & A whenever you like. If it happens to be just after you've given a response that will assure your firm of record profits next year, well, that's just the way it happened, isn't it?

Isn't it?

CHAPTER

Nuts & Bolts:
Practical Skills for Presenters

◆ ◆ ◆

*"Nothing in life is so exhilarating as to be shot at
without result."*
— WINSTON CHURCHILL

64 ▸ Food, Caffeine, and Energy

What's your drug of choice as a speaker?

Is it coffee?

Some pre-speech cans of Coca-Cola?

A mind-numbing martini or three?

If you're looking for focus, dynamism, and power as a speaker, your energy source should be *proper breathing* rather than any of the usual suspects named above. That, along with solid preparation and practice, will bring you to the peak of performance you're seeking.

It's not such a stretch to believe that sufficient breathing is necessary to fully activate the vocal cords and project sound outward to listeners. But what about the rest of our physical performance as presenters? What can give us enough of a boost to be lively and animated from our first word to our last?

The natural answer is carbohydrates.

The *artificial* answer is caffeine.

Both can play a role in energizing our presentation persona.

Carbohydrates: If you're a devotee of a low-carbohydrate or no-carbohydrate diet, you're putting yourself at an energy disadvantage as a public speaker. Protein is unequalled for building tissue, but it doesn't provide a reliable and predictable source of energy the way carbohydrates do.

Here's how our body's energy-producing factory works: What ultimately gives us energy as a presenter (aside from our passion for our topic and our excitement in the speaking situation) is sugar. This is good news—at least for non-diabetics—since it is easy for us to control the level of sugar in our bloodstream.

Simple sugars such as refined sugar, orange juice, candy, etc., produce energy immediately. And *complex carbohydrates* such as pasta, bread, rice, etc., turn into sugar gradually as our body processes them.

By taking in a combination of simple sugars and complex carbohydrates, we can provide ourselves with an ongoing energy supply throughout our presentation. The orange juice and sugar in our tea at breakfast gives us an immediate boost, and the toast or pastries we also had provide an ongoing energy supply for the next 2-3 hours.

(Be aware, however, that fat-laden sugary foods such as chocolate bars and other rich confections can slow us down, since our body processes fats very slowly.)

Caffeine: If you also depend upon caffeine to provide your Oomph Factor, know that a time lag operates between the ingestion of your beverage of choice and its energy benefits. Caffeine reaches its full effect only after an hour, and continues to perform its magic for up to 4 hours after ingestion.[6]

So if you were up all night preparing and you're depending upon that gallon of coffee to pry your eyes open, keep this relatively long lead time in mind.

If, on the other hand, caffeine turns you into Mr. or Ms. Hyde, time your last injection so that it will *wear off* before you get up to speak.

All systems go, then?

"10, 9, 8, 7, 6 . . ."

65   How to Speak from Notes Or a Manuscript

It isn't difficult to read from notes or a manuscript in a speech while still relating to your listeners.

Why then do so many people do it badly? It can't be because speakers find it fruitful to pretend that there's no one actually *listening* to their speeches. And it can't possibly help to have a closer relationship with your speaking notes than with your audience.

After all, if the whole idea behind a presentation is to influence one's listeners, a speaker had better find a way to establish rapport with that audience! (Are *you* willing to be influenced by someone who basically denies your existence?)

What follows are six practical tips for speaking effectively while using a manuscript or notes. These suggestions will help you remain engaging and influential as a speaker while maintaining a conversational dynamic with your listeners. (Incidentally, I favor an "extemporaneous" style of speaking using keywords or phrases instead of an entire manuscript, but there are situations

---

[6] Baker and Theologus 1972, Quoted in Anthony P. Winston, Elizabeth Hardwick, and Neema Jaberi, "Neuropsychiatric effects of caffeine," Advances in Psychiatric Treatment 2005 (vol. 11, 433). (Accessed 22 January 2007 at http://apt.rcpsych.org/cgi/reprint/11/6/432.pdf.)

in which a prepared text is necessary.)

1. **Write to Speak.** Compose your talk for the *ears*—not the eyes—of your listeners. Aim for the rhythms of conversation rather than the more formal style of memos and reports (or the barely-composed slang of e-mail messages). That means simple words and short sentences. Use a tape recorder to listen to yourself to improve in this area.

2. **Make it Easy to Read.** Give yourself pages that are easy for you to see from the lectern. Use a large typeface, wide margins, and avoid the bottom of the page (otherwise your audience will see the top of your head too often).

3. **Grab and Run With Key Phrases.** You don't want to spend more time with your text than with your listeners. So look down and "grab" key phrases or sentences. Then look up at your listeners and say them. Practice the technique to acquire a rhythm, for this is an essential skill for speakers. An important general rule: *If you're not LOOKING at your audience, nothing should be coming out of your mouth.*

4. **Use the Pause That Refreshes.** That's an old ad slogan, but it applies for public speakers—who must learn to use pauses! Pauses help shape your speech. They show that you're confident enough to let an idea sit there, and then sink in. They are refreshing for listeners. Adrenalin will be prodding you to *speed up,* but you must take time to pause. A speech without pauses seems to go on forever, regardless of its actual length.

5. **Look at Your Listeners.** This is the forest that speakers don't see, because the trees that made the pages of their manuscript are getting in the way. You must look up from your speech *with every sentence you say.* Audience members need eye contact to believe you're talking to *them;* and none of us is persuaded by someone who won't look us in the eye.

6. **Reach Your Peaks.** Remember that your speech or presentation needs *shape*, in terms of both ideas and vocal delivery. A speech lacking a climax, for instance, is as formless and anony-

mous as an amoeba; and presentations without vocal variety are sheer torture for listeners. The tendency of our voice to "flatten out" increases when we read from a notes or a manuscript, rather than converse with listeners. Remind yourself in every instance that you are talking to people, not sheets of paper. People demand much more from you than lifeless words on a page. But provided you *breathe life* into those words—your listeners will return the favor handsomely.

66 Surviving an Encounter with a Wild Lectern

If you've read this far in this book, chances are you're aware that speaking in public can be exhilarating and rewarding. In fact, delivering a key speech or presentation can be career-enhancing in ways that few endeavors are.

There's another side to public speaking, however. The dark truth is that there are speech-related objects and props that will eat you alive if given half a chance.

Note cards, projectors, laptops, and microphones all fall in this category. But for sheer aggression and potential for lasting damage, nothing beats the lectern.

The lectern! The very symbol of public humiliation and thwarted ambitions! Rapport-destroying barricade! (Don't be fooled by its frequent masquerading as a "podium" either—as though it was that harmless platform that you can safely stand on.)

No, lecterns are those big blocky monsters that prevent access to listeners (and vice-versa), and love to gobble speakers whole.

But do not despair. Here are 5 Essential Rules of Survival that you should follow, if you find yourself locked in mortal combat with one of these voracious creatures:

Survival Rule # 1 – Keep both feet planted firmly on the floor, even if your audience can't see them. If you lean on one leg—or worse, cross your feet—you will look and feel unstable. That's bad enough. But lecterns have been known to *bite off* the appendages of people who leave a foot or leg wandering on its own.

Survival Rule #2 – Gesture frequently with your hands and arms *so the lectern doesn't realize you're scared.* If you remain perfectly still, a mature lectern will either: a) think you are made of wood like it is, and attempt to absorb you completely; or b) realize that you are frozen in place from fear and therefore unable to defend yourself. It will then immediately initiate hostile actions.

Survival Rule # 3 – If you make the unwise choice to keep your arms completely still, at least *place one hand lightly on either side of your manuscript.* Don't let your hands disappear completely from view (see Rule #1 about vulnerable appendages). Leaning heavily on the lectern itself, on the other hand, will make you appear truculent or drunk, and the added pressure will make the lectern very angry.

Survival Rule # 4 – Do not grasp the front or sides of a lectern with a grip that turns your knuckles white. Apparently, white knuckles appear to be a particular delicacy for lecterns.

Survival Rule # 5 – Step away from the lectern occasionally if the speech situation allows it. It will help your engagement with your audience if you can eliminate the physical barrier between you and them. But much more critically... you'll have a head start of a step or two if those jaws open wiiiide.

67   Testing... Testing... Is This Thing On?

Microphones make speakers nervous, and for good reason. Something weird happens to our voices when we're miked. It's called *amplification*. Human beings, after all, were not meant to sound like Zeus, Broadway theaters notwithstanding. Miking makes our voices sound electronic, and that understandably makes us uneasy. We've evolved so that we're comfortable listening to people speak through the medium of air, not amplified electrical current.

Microphones also diminish a speaker's physical presence—along with the wonderful array of physical clues that go into expressing ourselves. We used to communicate publicly with other people in large open spaces—fields, marketplaces and public squares, the rotundas of enormous stone buildings, and so on.

To be an effective speaker in these environments, one needed to bring one's *entire presence* to the communication process. Vocal strength and projection, facial expressions, gestures, movement, and the sheer need to *reach out* to one's listeners—all these factors came into play as we launched our messages across the physical space that separated us from our listeners.

With amplified sound, none of those elements are necessary, aside from the voice—and even then, the voice has to be diminished so as not to overpower the auditor.

The challenge for you when you use a microphone as a speaker, then, is to keep the essential interaction between you and your listeners, even though you can't call on some of the tools you're accustomed to use in doing so! Your primary relationship with your audience hasn't changed, even if the microphone tempts you to ignore the physical components of an effective speech performance.

All of this is to make the argument that you should ignore the microphone if you're forced to use one, and give your presentation as if it wasn't even there.

Don't worry about adequate volume for instance. That's the job of the sound technician (or all-around AV person at the company). There's no need for you to lean in to a mic to make yourself heard. Talk at your normal volume, though you mustn't of course wander so far away from the mic that your voice disappears.

At its best, a microphone is there to make what you're saying audible and intelligible, and that's all. Achieving the level of influence you want—as in everything else I've said in this book—means being your true and honest self. In particular, it means giving the type of presentation you're comfortable with, and not changing anything because of one piece of technology.

Being a credible, trustworthy, and dynamic speaker is challenging enough. You don't need a microphone changing who you are on the way to that goal.

68   The Four Golden Rules for Using PowerPoint

In the spirit of making every PowerPoint presentation a tool of enlightenment rather than an instrument of torture, here are Four Golden Rules for Using PowerPoint.

You will no doubt notice that the first letters of the Rules spell "GIVE." I have no idea how that happened, but I'm glad it did! After all, we "give" a speech, don't we? Similarly, these rules will help you "give" your listeners helpful information instead of "giving" them a nervous breakdown.

Here's how you can do so:

Give Them Time. Audiences become confused when a presenter shows a slide with a significant amount of information, and then talks over the slide by saying something different. The brain is then forced to ask itself: "Do I read the written information or listen to what's being said?"

It's your job as a presenter, of course, to build on or amplify the information on your slides. But to do that, you need to let your audience members read what you're showing them before you start talking about it. After all, they've never seen this slide before and need time to absorb it. Give them that time. By reading the information silently to yourself, you'll know exactly when you should start speaking.

Introduce Your Slides. A terrific way to increase anticipation and interest in your upcoming slide is to "introduce" it. That is, rather than simply clicking to the next slide and launching into discussing it, use transitions to link what you've just been talking about, to what's coming up next.

Here's an example: "Okay, we've looked at our long-term goals in launching Super-Profitable-Thing II. Now, how can we create buzz in the marketplace before it hits the shelves?" And your next slide, titled, "Creating Some Buzz!" shows some of those ways. Now your presentation has a more logical structure and is easier to understand.

Vary Your Rate of Presentation. Audience members become anesthetized by an endless line of slides flashing by like billboards on a dark highway. But all slides are not created equal. Some are more important than others, and warrant more time and attention spent on them.

Invest yourself in your critical slides, and move more quickly through supporting slides. If possible, include some other components in your talk besides PowerPoint to help break up the rate and tempo of your presentation. Group activities, demonstrations, exercises, even a short survey, are ways to achieve some variety. Which brings us to the final Rule:

Engage Your Audience. Find ways to step out of your PowerPoint show and actively invite responses from your listeners, especially if your presentation is a long one. Quick Tip #43 ("The Best Kept Secret of PowerPoint") discusses one of these ways: using the "B" or "black" button. The B-button brings your screen to black, so your audience *has* to look back at you.

Even with your current slide still showing, however, you can ask questions, tell an interesting anecdote, challenge or cajole your audience, hand out a visual aid, etc., etc., etc. As your high school art teacher used to say, "You're only limited by your imagination."

69 Jokes, Humor, and Other Serious Stuff

I don't know whether the chicken or the egg came first—but I *do* know that this question preceded both:

"Should I start my presentation with a joke?"

Well, in fowl weather or fair, it all depends.

Humor can be an entertaining and persuasive public speaking tool. But unless people laugh good-naturedly whenever you enter a room, you shouldn't give humor the central role in your talk. That advice even holds for after-dinner speeches, which are supposed to be entertaining. Any humor in your speeches still has to serve the message you're imparting, just like every other element of your talk.

Let's look at how humor can help you to speaking success, and the places where the ice gets a little thin.

Jeff Fleming said this recently in the pages of *Professional Speaker,* the journal of the National Speakers Association: "Humor makes an audience more receptive to your message, improves retention of points made, reduces tension, improves creativity and provides entertainment value to any presentation." [7]

Pretty effective stuff, humor! We might also add: Humor allows your audience to see that you're human and to identify with you. And it lets everybody in the room have some fun as well.

Like any presentation tool, however, humor must be used judiciously, and in the context of your message. Here's an exam-

---

[7] Jeff Fleming, "Observational Humor: Seeing What Others Are Thinking," *Professional Speaker,* November 2005, 10.

ple of what happens when those two considerations *aren't* taken into account:

A year or so ago, I conducted a workshop at a large multinational manufacturer. Senior executives of nearly a dozen departments were represented, from finance to distribution. On the workshop's second day, each participant was required to give a 10-minute presentation which we videotaped and discussed afterwards. One of the executives started his speech with a joke. Now, this was a stretch-limo of a joke, since it took him $3\frac{1}{2}$ minutes of his allotted 10 minutes to get to the punch line. Even worse, the joke was about the *Pope!*

How's that for living dangerously?

This brief true story contains four valuable lessons about how to use humor in presentations:

1. The humor shouldn't take up so much time that it competes with the body of your presentation.
2. The humor should be culturally appropriate to your audience. In other words, you should have a reasonable idea that it's safe. Who knows, for instance, how many Catholics may sit in this man's future audiences, and be offended by a joke about the Pope?
3. The humor must be *closely related* to your topic. In the above case, the presenter labored mightily to tie his punch line with the topic that followed, but it was an impossible task.
4. Using humor is usually productive, while telling a *joke* is inviting T-R-O-U-B-L-E. There's a world of difference, that is, between relating a humorous story your audience can relate to, and handing them a zinger of a sidesplitting gag.

Telling a joke well requires timing, the ability to assume voices and characterizations, and the honed skills of a stand-up comic. These needs are usually worlds apart from the credibility you must achieve with business and professional audiences.

So keep it safe and in good taste—just like the products from the Good Humor Man.

70 When Your Audience Has Eaten a Bowling Ball for Lunch

Unless you have a death wish, I suggest you object to giving your presentation immediately after lunch. This slot is second only to being the speaker just *before* lunch in the Presentation Horrors Hall of Fame.

The world of business speeches and presentations being what it is, however, there will be times when you're asked to speak in either of these situations. My advice for the before-lunch slot is simple and straightforward: shorten your presentation by one-third from the schedule you were given. This will keep *you* from being the entrée, and you may even get an extra slice of dessert for your niceness.

My advice for the post-prandial presentation requires more discussion.

So what can you do when each audience member's blood supply has fled from brain to belly to handle the all-too-common conference meal of prime rib, rich mashed potatoes, buttery green beans, cheesecake, and coffee-with-half-and-half? (I'm assuming, of course, that you yourself have dined lightly on car-bohydrates to provide you with a continuing source of energy over the next couple of hours. Yes?)

In such dire circumstances, you must think *activity*.

This is a generous continuum that embraces everything from stimulating creative thinking, to getting your audience on its feet for calisthenics. And I'm not kidding! I routinely have C-level executives and United Nations ambassadors performing jumping jacks.

The one thing you don't want your audience to be allowed to do is to settle comfortably into their seats, while your presentation glides by like an unthreatening dream in a pleasant nap.

Instead, let your audience know that it's not safe when you're in the room. *Insist* on participation—mental or physical (or both)—right at the start of your talk. Pose a rhetorical question. Better yet, ask a real question that requires a response.

You might ask everyone to interact with the person on their right (e.g., "Introduce yourself and tell that person what your job is within the company" still works if you make it sound like fun). Or break your listeners up into groups (that's right—you can do so even this early in your presentation).

Distribute a short survey. Ask for a volunteer to demonstrate something (believe me, seeing your gaze travel over the audience as you look for said "volunteer" will *really* wake everyone up!). Or just get them on their feet for a good stretch. That simple technique can be an effective one when everybody is fighting off the drowsies.

Remember, your presentation is always about *engaging* your listeners in every way possible. That objective just needs a little extra help when Bowling Ball Tartar is on the menu.

71 Tips for Preparation and Practice

Now that you've followed all the other advice in this book, you're ready to gather up your materials and give a dynamic and influential presentation. It should be an enjoyable experience for you and your audience.

And if the stars align—it could be a turning point in your career or your organization's success.

But like all great things, the nuts-and-bolts preparation you do beforehand is what will ensure your eventual success. In that spirit, here are three pieces of practical advice for "getting ready" with your speech, presentation, or talk.

There's one bit of wisdom I'd like to share with you first, though. It's the best advice I know of for becoming a more accomplished presenter:

Acquire as much speaking experience as possible.

Take *every* opportunity to speak in public—even if that's a nerve-racking proposition for you. That's the only way to gain control over your fear, and to reach that state of mind in which speaking in front of others is both a pleasurable and productive activity for you.

Now, the practical advice:

1. **Prepare solid briefing materials:** Take a page from diplomats and other public affairs types and put together a briefing book. Ask yourself these questions as you compile your information:

◆ Are my materials memorable (for *me*)?
◆ Have I anticipated questions and objections?
◆ Does each of my main points "headline" the information to come?
◆ Is my information well laid out and visually highlighted for my benefit?

2. **Plan your practice sessions:** A good strategy for your practice sessions can be just as helpful as visualizing success in your presentation itself. Here's how to go about it:

◆ **Timing:** Begin sooner rather than later: Give yourself sufficient time!
◆ **Emphasis:** Be clear on what you're focusing on. For instance, are you looking for feedback on your content? Logic and language? Level of audience interaction? Visual

components?

♦ **Setting:** Go from rough-and-ready settings to as close an approximation as you can of the real situation, venue, and audience.

♦ **Post-Performance Feedback:** Define for yourself what you'll consider a success, and let subordinates and colleagues know that you expect and welcome criticism.

♦ **Rehearse 3 to 5 times:** Less than three times is almost winging it. If you rehearse more than 5 times, you'll run the risks of a) becoming stale; and b) memorizing movements and consciously repeating them so that you look mechanical.

3. **Have an out-of-body experience:** Videotape yourself, or use a tape recorder if you'll be speaking on radio. Watch, listen, and work on the rough spots. It's as simple as that.

You need to hear and see yourself as others experience you. The modern miracle of electronic equipment allows you to do that. Make use of it!

72   A Checklist of Nonverbal Delivery Skills

Body Language: Was my body language effective?
☐ Did I demonstrate a confident yet relaxed posture?
☐ Did I include natural-looking movement while avoiding repetitive gestures?
☐ Were my gestures supportive of what I was saying?
☐ Was my face expressive of my ideas and emotions?
☐ Did I make direct and ongoing eye contact?

Vocal Qualities: Was my voice interesting and dynamic?
☐ Did I vary my pitch and speak at a reasonable tempo?
☐ Was my vocal tone pleasant and confident-sounding?

☐ Did I sound intellectually and emotionally committed to my ideas?

☐ Was my voice lively and energetic?

☐ Did I use pauses to let my messages sink in?

Use of Space: Did I command the space in which I spoke and moved?

☐ Did I "own" my space, not diminishing or over-expanding my physical presence?

☐ Was my movement fluid rather than abrupt or jerky?

☐ Did I sit or stand poised and ready, without slouching?

☐ Was I open (not closed off) physically?

☐ Was I animated instead of stiff and wooden?

73 Lies, Damn Lies, and Statistics

> *"Father, I cannot tell a lie: In the Colonies, fully*
> *37.8% of boys cut down a cherry tree as a normal part*
> *of adolescent development."*
> — WHAT GEORGE WASHINGTON REALLY SAID

Among the educational gems I remember from high-school is one from Mr. McDevitt's 10th grade Economics class. He warned us to be careful of statistics. The exact same data, he told us, can be used to justify any position—including those that are directly opposed to each other.

I can certainly think of a political position or two that appear to prove Mr. McDevitt's argument.

Mark Twain said all of this another way. As he wrote in his *Autobiography* (though he attributed the remark to Benjamin Disraeli): "There are three kinds of lies—Lies, damn lies, and statistics."

For our purpose as speakers, we must bear in mind yet another characteristic of these numerical pieces of evidence: By themselves, statistics are cold, hard things. For our audiences to relate to them and take them to heart, the statistics we use must be *humanized*.

Put another way: people will generally only remember a statistic if it is attached to human experiences and emotions—such as their own.

Let's take an example. Suppose you're giving a talk with an anti-smoking message. You could simply say, "Smoking-related diseases claim an estimated 440,000 American lives each year,"[8] and leave it at that.

Or you can start out the same way, but continue thus: "Smoking-related diseases claim an estimated 440,000 American lives each year. That's a big number—but what does it mean in terms we can relate to? Well, that's the equivalent of a fully-loaded 747 airliner crashing, with every soul onboard killed, every single day for 884 days, or *two-and-a-half years*."

I guarantee that the second version would have more impact.

Another way to make your statistic vivid in listeners' minds is to bring it from the macro to the micro level. Here, you frame the overwhelming statistic in terms of a single life or a few lives. To stay with our health theme, for example: Suppose your message is how thousands of women's lives could be saved each year by monthly breast self-examinations.

Rather than just throw out your statistic, you could start out with the story of a single woman. Immediately following your greeting, that is, you could say: "On October 16, 1996, Melissa S. Dougherty noticed a small lump in her right breast. She was only 31 years old—a wife and mother of two toddlers—so she didn't think too much of it. The truth is she was also a little

---

[8] http://www.lungusa.org/site/pp.asp?c=dvLUK9O0E&b=39853, 9 March 2006.

afraid. Three more months went by as Melissa ignored the lump, until finally her husband noticed it because of its increasing size. It was Jack Dougherty who convinced Melissa to go to the doctor."

From there, you lead into your message of why monthly breast self-exams are critical to women's survival rates.* The biggest payoff would come, of course, if there is a personal connection between you as speaker and the statistic: if you, for instance, are the woman in the story. But it isn't necessary.

And even if such a connection doesn't exist, speaking in terms of human beings rather than grand statistics will make your numbers hit home when you finally reveal them. That way, you'll be ensuring that your vital statistic goes home with your listeners.

74 ◆ 7 Tips for a Successful Job Interview

As you know, or should know, a successful job search is only partly about the interview itself. Other behavior that you exhibit is equally important. These critical situations include your phone skills in setting up the interview; your prompt and professional follow up to the meeting; any personal connections that can bolster your candidacy, and so on.

That said, your interaction with your interviewer(s) remains the single most important factor in landing a job. Here are seven suggestions for standing out from the crowd as you seek that dream position:

1. **Show Confidence.** Your interviewers have brought you in because they genuinely want to know who you are and how

---

* If you use this technique, you must of course let your audience know what eventually happened with "Melissa Dougherty." Bring her in again at the end of your talk, when you reveal how Melissa was lucky—and how breast self-exams are critical for keeping more women from finding themselves in her situation.

you might fit into their organization. They'll have a hard time figuring any of this out if you sit blandly, responding robot-like to their questions.

Have the confidence and courage to be you. That means taking your responses into your territory, not merely following the crumbs to where you think they want you to go. Your interviewers know you're probably nervous. Exhibiting sufficient self-esteem will differentiate you from all the other candidates who come across as *just* nervous.

2. **Initiate.** When you walk into your interviewer's office, be the one to initiate the moment of greeting. "So nice to meet you. Thank you for having me here today," is a great opener, for instance. Showing enough initiative to reach out first is a very good sign. So act rather than react.

3. **Notice and Comment.** What is there in the room or situation that you can comment on? Do you have a mutual acquaintance or hobby? Is the view from the window stunning? What about that intriguing Balinese mask on the wall?

Remember: most applicants will simply arrive, sit down, and begin taking questions. What's memorable about that? If you make an intelligent and appropriate comment to start out, you'll be remembered. Now take a seat once you're invited to, and keep in mind the following points as you speak:

4. **Organization and Logic.** Show that you've invested some thought in this industry, company, and your possible place in the scheme of things. Try to make it appear that you're a self-starter with a nimble mind.

Make your points concisely and back them up with evidence. Be firm without being dogmatic; generous when mentioning others; personable but not silly. Impress them with the value of your opinions, without seeming to consider them worthy of Fort Knox.

5. **Enthusiasm.** Convey the impression that this employment opportunity excites you. Project enough energy that they

pick up on it and get a charge themselves. They'll feel good about the interview afterwards, even if they can't put their finger on exactly why.

6. **Emotion. Be human.** Don't buy into the myth that emotions have no place in the world of business and commerce. Be passionate about the things that matter to you (as long as you don't come across as obsessive). Just be sure that your passionate positions are in line with their thinking and business practices.

7. **Smile.** We smile too infrequently in our professional lives. If this job interview appears to be making you work like hell, it'll seem like hard work for your interviewers too. They may even get the subliminal impression that the thought of being part of this organization doesn't turn you on. Instead of leading them to such a grim conclusion, try to seem like a pleasant person to be around.

Most of all, don't be a mysterious presence who needs information coaxed out of them, grunt by inconclusive response. That works for Hollywood anti-heroes and comic book crime-fighters, but not for the rest of us.

75 Toasts, Awards, Testimonials, and Other Special Occasions

Speeches on special occasions can provoke greater anxiety than everyday, business-related speaking assignments. Yet the truth is that a request to speak at these events is an honor. Our position, closeness to the people or events being feted, or our distinction in our field is responsible for our place of prominence on the occasion.

That special knowledge or experience is what you should draw upon as you prepare and deliver your special occasion speech.

Tell the stories that *these* listeners will find interesting. In particular, reveal your personal connection with the honoree(s). But most of all—be honest. What the audiences at these events want is sincerity, not polish.

Recently, one of my wife's relatives died in his early fifties, leaving his mother and three siblings. At his wake, the family asked me to read the eulogy his brothers and sister had written, the following day at the funeral mass. They reasoned that I would do a good job because of my background as an actor.

I told them I would be happy to do so if they insisted, but that I felt it would mean much more to everyone if one of them read the eulogy. Eventually they agreed. And though the brother who spoke the words was not a polished speaker, he tapped into bittersweet emotions for the relatives that I'd never have been able to approach.

When it comes to public speaking on special occasions, honesty trumps show business every time. It isn't the wisdom of the ages your listeners are hoping for—it's *you*. So be confident in your worth as a valued contributor, and speak from the heart.

Here is some specific advice concerning different occasions:

◆ **The Toast.** Eloquence is expected here. That doesn't mean that you must suddenly morph into a New York sophisticate. If you stay simple and true, conveying your honest affection for the honoree(s), *you will be eloquent*. This is also an ideal place to use quotations, either from people known to the listeners or famous persons. A word to the wise: Beware of alcohol, which may be flowing freely at your table by the time you stand to speak.

◆ **The Roast.** Introduce yourself if you aren't known to everyone in the room. A general rule of roasts is that the closer you are to the "roastee," the further in you can slip your blade—all in good fun, of course. Remember that self-deprecating humor is always welcome at a roast, since it shows that you can take it as well as dish it out.

◆ **Master of Ceremonies.** Maintain a firm but light touch. Don't make the mistake of thinking that just because you've been invited to be the MC, this is about you. It isn't. Learn the names and titles of the people you're introducing and then let them do their own thing. Perhaps most important: speak beforehand with your host to see what he or she wants you to do. Then give exactly that—no more and no less. And be sure you know how you're expected to dress.

◆ **Blessing, Grace, or Benediction.** A successful blessing combines the true and eternal with the particular. Prayers and profound thoughts from the Bible, poetry, and the wisdom of other religions and cultures are always appropriate. Bear in mind that we can also go outside the "expected" sources if we find something appropriate and refreshing. A beautiful feature of a prayer, for instance, can be our own addition, something original that we've thought up for the occasion. That's a way to take the eternal and link it to the special occasion of the gathering.

◆ **Acceptance Speech or Response to a Testimonial.** Here, less is definitely more. Nothing sours an audience's goodwill more quickly than a too-long or self-indulgent acceptance speech. Think Oscars, and you'll know exactly what I mean. So: humbly thank your sponsors, mention others as accomplished as you who didn't win the award, and make a graceful exit.

◆ **Eulogy.** The sometimes surprising truth about eulogies is that they don't have to be sad and somber set-pieces. Eulogies represent a wonderful opportunity for all present to *celebrate the life* of the person, not just mourn their passing. Here again, heartfelt emotion is the key. I gave the eulogy at my mother's funeral, and I had to stop speaking more than once because emotion overtook me and closed my throat. But I simply paused, collected myself, and went on. At one point I even thanked everyone for being so patient!

If you deliver a eulogy, find a way to tap into the joy that this person's life made possible. In the movie *Mr. Saturday Night*, Billy Crystal's character—a professional comedian—gives a hilarious and bittersweet eulogy at his mother's funeral. The fact that everyone is laughing throughout his presentation in no way diminishes the deep affection the survivors have, and are busy showing, for the deceased.

◆ ◆ ◆

Gary Genard, Ph.D., is an internationally known expert in communication performance. A former professional actor, he helps clients worldwide excel in speaking skills for leadership, advocacy, and business success. Dr. Genard consults for Fortune 500 companies, trade associations, the United Nations, the U.S. Congress and State Department, NGOs, consulting firms, and executives worldwide. Contact him at www.publicspeakinginternational.com.